In the Path of the Storms

In the

Photo by Adrian Overstreet © MOC 2005

Path of the Storms

Bayou La Batre, Coden, and the Alabama Coast

Frye Gaillard, Sheila Hagler, and Peggy Denniston

A Pebble Hill Book

Published with The University of Alabama Press

Printed in Canada.

The paper on which this book is printed meets the minimum requirements of American National Standard for Information Science—Permanence of Paper for Printed Library Materials, ANSI Z39.48-1984

Jimmy Wigfield's story in the appendix Bayou Voices is copyright 2007 by the *Mobile Register.*

The poems by Jada Davis and Saphea Khan and the essay by Peggy Denniston appearing in Bayou Voices are copyright 2006 by Merging of Cultures.

The excerpt from *Whistlin' Woman and Crowin' Hen* is copyright 1956 by Julian Lee Rayford.

In the Path of the Storms is published by Pebble Hill Books, Auburn University, Auburn, Alabama, and The University of Alabama Press, Tuscaloosa, Alabama.

Pebble Hill Books is an imprint series published by the Caroline Marshall Draughon Center for the Arts & Humanities in collaboration with the University of Alabama Press. The Center is the outreach office of the College of Liberal Arts at Auburn University. Titles in the series grow out of or contribute to its outreach mission. Special thanks to the Kettering Foundation of Ohio for its support of this book.

Special thanks to the *Journal of American History*

Library of Congress Cataloging-in-Publication Data

Gaillard, Frye, 1946–
    In the path of the storms : Bayou La Batre, Coden, and the Alabama coast /
Frye Gaillard, Sheila Hagler, and Peggy Denniston.
        p. cm.
        "A Pebble Hill Book."
    Includes bibliographical references.
    ISBN 978-0-8173-5504-3 (pbk. : alk. paper) — ISBN 978-0-8173-8073-1 (electronic)
1. La Batre, Bayou (Ala.) — History. 2. Coden (Ala.) — History. 3. Fishing villages — Alabama —
History. 4. La Batre, Bayou (Ala.) — Ethnic relations. 5. Coden (Ala.) — Ethnic relations. 6. Southeast
Asian Americans — Alabama — Gulf Coast — History. 7. Hurricane Katrina, 2005. I. Hagler, Sheila.
II. Denniston, Peggy. III. Title.
    F334.B36G24 2008
    976.1'22 — dc22
                                                                                        2007038380

To the memory of Floyd Bosarge and Jada Davis,

whose lives embodied the tradition and the hope

Contents

Preface   ix

Introduction — Life on the Edge   3

1 The Storytellers   9

2 The Refugees   29

3 Katrina   47

4 The Long Road Back   65

Appendix — Bayou Voices   89

Notes and Acknowledgments   117

Preface

This book grew out of an article for the *Journal of American History*, first presented at "Through the Eye of Katrina," a national conference of historians held in the early spring of 2007. In cooperation with the University of South Alabama, which hosted the conference, the *JAH* decided to publish a special edition on Hurricane Katrina and the historical impact of that catastrophe.

Most of the articles centered, quite properly, on the city of New Orleans, where the complexity and poignancy of that community's experience are likely to be studied for decades to come. But the *Journal*'s editor, Ed Linenthal, asked me to write a supplementary piece on the Alabama coast, particularly the village of Bayou La Batre, which represented, in a sense, the eastern edge of the Katrina disaster. In writing that story, I discovered a rich and complicated culture, a town simultaneously old and new. It was a place where history was alive and well, where people told stories of past generations who had extracted a modest living from the sea.

These traditions represented a powerful force, an anchor for a deep, pervasive sense of place that I discovered I wanted to explore more fully. At about the same time, the Caroline Marshall Draughon Center for the Arts & Humanities in the College of Liberal Arts at Auburn University, an important institution in the intellectual life of this state, was expanding a community history project funded by the Kettering Foundation of Ohio and undertaken in collaboration with AU's Truman

Pierce Institute. Focusing on how a community's history influences its present, the project was a perfect fit for Bayou La Batre. I was fortunate also to make the acquaintance of Sheila Hagler and Peggy Denniston, two artists in residence in the Mobile County schools who were already working with students and families to help them come to terms with the disaster.

With the convergence of all these resources, I have been able to spend the better part of a year interviewing residents of Coden and Bayou La Batre—adjacent communities bound together by history, geography, culture, and family—and I have sifted through the written record of the area. Hagler and Denniston, who know the place well, have added their insights, as well as photographs—Hagler's own, plus those taken by their students and other residents of the Bayou area. I have written the main text, and together we have compiled what is probably the most important part of the book: a collection of Bayou Voices, first-person recollections from people, including Denniston, who live and work in this fascinating place.

We believe the result is a powerful story. In addition to the literal fury of Katrina, the Bayou has been hit in the past quarter century by the winds of cultural and economic change, and the shape of its future is not at all clear.

As the community struggles with its new challenges, we hope this book, in some modest way, will be of benefit to the process. The people of the Bayou—white, black, and Asian—know who they are, and we believe that with the right leadership, they will build on a deeply felt sense of tradition rather than see it destroyed. We wish them the best.

—Frye Gaillard

In the Path of the Storms

Bayous large and small crisscross the area around Bayou La Batre.

Introduction—*Life on the Edge*

About once a century in Bayou La Batre, catastrophic storms come roaring in from the Gulf. Ninety-nine years before Katrina, there was the hurricane of 1906, a mighty wind that lasted for more than twenty-four hours, long before these events had names. The memories of that storm linger even now in the oral history of the Bayou—in the family stories handed down for generations in this fishing village on the Alabama coast.

Alma Bryant, a girl of thirteen in 1906, and later her community's leading educator, remembered being separated from her family as the tidal surge tore her house from its moorings. "Rain, the coldest and heaviest I have ever felt, pounded me relentlessly," she said. "Then the vicious wind picked me up and immersed me in one of those craters made by an uprooted tree. I clutched the limb . . . and held on for dear life, barely conscious of the weird noises all around me—the shrieks of frightened birds, the woeful cry of a drowning calf, the dying moans of Mr. Deakle's old white mare pinned beneath the demolished barn."

Miss Bryant, in the end, was one of the lucky ones. She managed to swim and clamber through the floating debris—"the limp, dead chickens, bloated hogs, writhing snakes"—toward the flickering light of a house in the distance. Many others didn't make it, and the *Mobile Register*, the morning newspaper in the nearest city, carefully recorded the details: two Bayou women lining up the bodies, covering them with shrouds; a frightened family emerging from the woods, where they had drifted all night in an open skiff; a writer's description of those who survived: "Most . . . resembled great chunks of liver-colored beef, so badly were they battered and bruised."

All of this is now part of the lore of Bayou La Batre, a place where residents freely acknowledge that life on the edge of the continent is hard. The hurricanes come and the hurricanes go, requiring resilience of those who survive. So it was in 1906, and so it has been after Hurricane Katrina. But there is another understanding more subtle and elusive, more difficult for people to explain. When the truly massive storms have hit the Bayou, the calamities that come only once a century or so, they have often changed the course of local history, much as they might alter the course of a river.

In the decade after 1906, a thriving tourist industry in Bayou La Batre and the contiguous coastal village of Coden began to shrink into almost nothing, as a string of turn-of-the-century resorts—the Rolston, the Oleander Hotel—closed their doors. The Bayou, in a sense, slowly but surely turned in on itself, returning to the source of its identity and survival: extracting its sustenance from the sea. The work was hard, but the people found satisfaction in the harvest—shrimp and oysters, fish and crabs, depending on the season. "We love it like a farmer loves digging in the dirt," says longtime oysterman Avery Bates. "You sweat hard and see the bounty of the sea, and you're part of a heritage going back for generations. You're feeding your family and the people around you. You know you're involved in something worthwhile."

But as Bates and others are now quick to tell you, the seafood industry has changed over time. The technology improved, and the catches grew large. But by the early years of the twenty-first century, higher fuel prices, competition from imported shrimp, and the growing complexity of government regulations had made many in the Bayou fear for the future of their profession. They had already lived through major upheavals, chief among them a massive immigration in the 1970s of Asian refugees—Laotians, Cambodians, and Vietnamese who were fleeing war and genocide in their homelands. These new arrivals had carved out a niche in the life and economy of Bayou La Batre, many of them working in the seafood industry, and soon they too faced an uncertain future.

As the global economy was changing around them, there was also the specter of high-end development—speculators who wanted to build new condominiums along the Bayou La Batre waterfront, displacing small-business owners in the process. "They are chomping at the bit to change this place," said a longtime shrimper whose family had lived in the town for a century. "A lot of ordinary people are going to be pushed aside."

It was against that backdrop that Hurricane Katrina came churning through the Gulf. In the warm, open waters, it reached the status of a Category 5, sending a massive storm swell surging toward the coast. On August 29, 2005, the water came ashore in Bayou La Batre, and in the lore of the place, there were suddenly new stories of terror and survival. Sophol and Chandara Ngam remembered the steady rise of the flood, filling their house, and still it wouldn't stop. They waded outside as the water kept coming, and kept getting deeper, and they knew that soon they would have to swim. But they didn't know how, and neither did most of their seven children. They began to call out, "No can swim! No can swim," and finally Ralph Harbison, a neighbor and volunteer fireman, appeared with a boat and carried them to safety.

Dozens of others had similar stories, reminiscent of disasters from an earlier time, and even when the waters began to recede, the horror of Hurricane Katrina remained. More than 2,000 people, out of a total population of 2,300, were forced from their homes, at least temporarily. Shrimp boats were tossed like driftwood into

Rodney Lyons, a
fifth-generation
Bayou resident,
opens oysters at a
shop he runs as
a family business.
© 2002 Sheila Hagler

the marsh, where they lay helpless and stranded for the next several months, and during that time one-fourth of the local residents moved away.

But Bayou La Batre had been there before. It had withstood the disasters down through the years, and even the more subtle forces of change, and there were many who believed it would do so again. "There really is a spirit about this place," said one volunteer who came to the Bayou just after Katrina. There were others, however, who were more apprehensive, people who had lived in the village all their lives and were worried about what the future might bring.

"If any of the development plans take hold," said onetime shrimper Randy Schjott, "it's going to change the face of this little shrimping village. I don't want to see that happen. There may be a few people get rich, but it won't replace the seafood shops or shipyards."

But Rodney Lyons, a fifth-generation Bayou resident who runs a tavern above his seafood brokerage, believed that, in the aftermath of Hurricane Katrina, the town had been presented with a new opportunity—an unexpected chance to focus on its future. "Katrina may have saved us," he said. Certainly it was true that in the months that followed the devastation of the storm, many local people began to ask questions: What kind of community did they want theirs to be? Was there a path to a stronger economic future that would still pay homage to the Bayou's traditions? Could people of different cultures work together?

As this book went to press, the answers to those questions were by no means clear. But to try to understand the gravity of the issues—the difficulties and hopes that were shaping the community in the wake of its latest natural disaster—it was necessary to go back in time, to talk to the people who had spent their lives on the Bayou, and to those who had arrived more recently. The result is a story of tradition and change, uncertainty and strength—the story of a place that, for all its flaws, takes hold of people's hearts and refuses to let go.

The shrimp boat
Margaret Ann
awaits her crew in
a Bayou harbor.

1 The Storytellers

Marie Gray's first memories were of the wind and the rain sweeping in from the Gulf, across Dauphin Island and the Mississippi Sound, and battering the little house where she lived. It was July 5, 1916, and Marie was only two years old. In the years since then, she has never been sure which pieces of the story she remembers on her own and which of them were simply told so often that they became a part of the picture in her mind. She knows that her father wasn't worried at first. He was a fisherman, after all, a man who had made his living from the sea, and he had seen his share of bad weather in the past.

But the surf was pounding on Coden beach, then surging across it, when a horse and buggy appeared at their door. It was Marie's aunt Clara, a local midwife and family matriarch, who had come to urge the others to leave right away. "It's a hurricane," she said. "Just get in the buggy and don't take anything. There isn't any time." Marie's mother glanced back at the dining room, where a cut-glass pitcher—a wedding present from a few years earlier—stood as a centerpiece on the table. There was nothing in her house that she valued more highly—nothing, of course, other than the members of her family, and she wondered what would be left when they returned.

Drenched and frightened as the wind hit its peak, they made their way to a house up the road, while the hurricane raged for most of a day. It was almost certainly a

Category 3—not quite as deadly as the storm of 1906, but devastating in its own right—part of a string of catastrophic storms that would ultimately destroy the tourist industry on the Bayou. The following morning, when the wind had slowed and the waters from the Gulf had begun to recede, Marie and her family returned to their homesite. Like the other residents of Coden beach, they discovered that there was nothing left at all.

"The whole house was gone," she said. "Everything was washed out to sea."

But then as they began to search through the rubble, among the underbrush and broken trees, they found the cut-glass pitcher that had been a wedding present. Somehow, remarkably, it was not even cracked, and the members of the family took it as a sign. It was their own little miracle from the storm, a symbol of continuity and survival, and when they built a new house further in from the beach, the pitcher took its place on the dining room table—a remnant of beauty for everyone to see.

When her parents died, Marie took it with her, and it became a prized possession in her life, a reminder of the past, as she began her work as a first-grade teacher. For nearly half a century, she taught at Alba school, and on Sundays for more than seventy years, she taught the children at her church in Coden. In her later years, after she retired, her private obsession became her garden, where she raised the most beautiful lilies in the town. And when at last she was too old for that, she would occasionally entertain visitors in her home, telling the stories of life on the Bayou—her mind as clear at the age of ninety-three as it had been in the days when she was teaching school.

Her family ties, she would explain, went all the way back to Joseph Bosarge, the village patriarch who secured a land grant in 1786 and built a home on the western shore of the bayou. When he settled next to this shallow estuary, which took its name, Bayou La Batre, from a battery of French cannons that had guarded the coastline, there were already Europeans just a few miles east, in what would eventually become known as Coden. Then as later, the whole area seemed to be of one piece, wooded and swampy, the waterways winding through savannahs of marsh grass and, immediately to the south, the open gray-blue waters of the Gulf.

It was also a place with a long human history, where the Indian people had lived for eight thousand years. They found abundant game in the forests—deer and bear, wild turkey and hogs—but their staples always came from the sea. Like the people who followed, the Native Americans shrimped and fished, gathered oysters and clams, and down through the years many scholars have marveled at the continuity of life on the bayou. Anthropologist Diane Silvia, writing in the *Gulf Coast Historical Quarterly*, argued that the coastal Indians were fundamentally different from the people further north. There, the intricately organized tribes—the Choctaws, Chickasaws, and Creeks—built their lives around farming, and by the time the Europeans arrived, they were living in larger communities and towns with all the interdependence that that required.

But down on the bayou, the Native Americans, like the new white settlers, grew accustomed to the self-sufficiency provided by their proximity to the sea—the venerated notion that a man and his family could make it on their own. Sometimes it was hard, especially when the storms blew in from the Gulf, but for anybody who was willing to work, there was pride and satisfaction to be had. In the view of many scholars, that is the story told by the archaeological record, and the story of the written history that followed.

That history began in the early 1700s when the French explorer Pierre LeMoyne Sieur d'Iberville began a series of expeditions to the area, laying claim to the land for King Louis XIV. One of the men in those expeditions, Jean-Baptiste Baudreau dit Graveline, fathered a son with an Indian woman he called Susanne.

A local
resident fishes
for his dinner
near the mouth
of the Bayou.
© 1998
Sheila Hagler

The mixed-blood son, whose name was Jean-Baptiste Baudreau, began a life of adventure along the Alabama coast that eventually led to his execution. Among other things, he seduced a teenaged girl whose family was living in what is now Coden. Books have been written about that affair, shrouding history with legend as people on this part of the coast often do. But the gist of the story seems to be as follows.

Sometime early in the 1740s, Baudreau found himself drawn to a beautiful girl, Henriette Huet, and their torrid affair produced two children, a girl and a boy. In 1744, facing a storm of community outrage, the couple decided to flee, and after stealing several slaves from Henriette's family, they took up residence among the Indians. By then Baudreau had earned a reputation as a rogue—a smuggler who often did business with the Spanish. But while the French officials saw him as a criminal, among the Indians he was always welcome. As one nineteenth-century historian would write, he "was often employed upon dangerous missions in the Creek nation and well understood the language of these Indians, besides that of neighboring tribes. . . . Baudreau was a powerful man, as to strength, and almost a giant in size, and these qualities, together with his bravery and prowess, endeared him to the Indians."

Eventually, however, Baudreau and Henriette left the Indians and sailed to Cuba, where they sought refuge among the Spanish. Instead, they were arrested and turned over to the French, where Baudreau was tried and sentenced to ten years as a galley slave in the navy. Henriette was allowed to return to her family, and soon thereafter married another man.

Baudreau, meanwhile, threw himself on the mercy of the king, pleading for a pardon, which was granted in 1747. But a decade later, he found himself in trouble once again. In 1757, he was accused—falsely, he insisted—of conspiring in the murder of a French official. Tried in Mobile, he was convicted along with one other man, and together they were executed on the wheel—the only time this grisly and medieval instrument of torture was ever to be used on American soil. The official report to the king of France described the executions this way: "On the 7th of last June, the man named Baudreau and the man named Joseph François Bazille . . . were sentenced to have their bodies broken, alive; to die upon the wheel; and to have their bodies cut into 4 pieces and thrown on the garbage dump, all of which had been carried out, in front of the troops, three hours after the sentence was handed down."

Baudreau left several children behind, at least two of whom, Pierre-Baptiste and Louise-Catherine, took up residence along the bayou. Louise, in fact, married Joseph Bosarge, founder and patriarch of what would soon become the largest and most prominent family in the town.

Joseph Bosarge, it seems, was far less colorful than Baudreau, though he too had lived through his share of melodrama. Born in Poitiers, France, probably in 1733, he had sailed to America as a young man and settled in the vicinity of Mobile. On June 5, 1762, he exchanged his vows with Louise Baudreau, and eighteen months later, when the British took control of the city, he pledged his allegiance to the new king. The first of seven children was born that year, and from all indications the family grew happily for the next eight years, until August 30, 1772, when a vicious hurricane swirled in from the Gulf, ruining their crops and flooding their home.

They moved to a bluff on the Tensaw River, and survived the turmoil of the American Revolution and the capture of Mobile by the Spanish in 1780. By 1786, however, the family had fallen on hard times, and Joseph, now approaching his sixtieth birthday, petitioned for a patch of bayou land. "Joseph Bouzage," he wrote, using one of several different spellings of his name, "has the honor to represent to your Excellency that he has been compelled in consequence of the state of his misery to retire with his wife and children on a piece of land situated on Bayou Batree . . . wherefore your petitioner dares to hope that his unfortunate situation will exercise the sense of your Excellency's feelings, and will be pleased to grant to him the said tract of land, in order that he may live thereon undisturbed, and to conceal from the eyes of everybody his poverty and misery, taking into consideration that he is a poor father of a family with seven children, who is troubled and his wife sickly."

It may well be that Joseph, in a plea for sympathy from the Spanish officials, exaggerated the state of his despair. If that was the case, it worked, for he was granted his title to the land, and eight days later, adaptable as ever, he swore his allegiance to the king of Spain.

In the years after that, the Bosarge family flourished and grew, providing an anchor for the village that soon grew up around them. They fished the bayous, tilled their acres of corn and other crops, and waged war against the wolves that threatened their cattle. (On May 29, 1820, according to Mobile County records, John Bosarge, a descendant of Joseph's, killed three wolves and was paid a bounty of fifteen dollars.) The Bayou was a rough-and-tumble place in those days and remained so through much of the century. Even much later, the old-timers would gather to tell their stories of pirates and ghosts and Saturday-night fights in the Bayou saloons.

In the 1950s, a Mobile author named Julian Rayford set out to write down some of those stories, and he stopped at the house of Uncle Bud Rabby, whose family was one of the first in Coden, just a few miles east of the Bosarge land. Uncle Bud himself came of age near the end of the nineteenth century, and he said his father-in-law had once killed a pirate.

"Killed a pirate?" said Rayford.

"He killed him dead," declared Uncle Bud. "Sure did! Killed him in a fistfight."

Uncle Bud went on to explain that back in 1837, give or take a couple of years, the pirate Spud Thompson had come ashore in Coden, spoiling for a fight. He found some local men at a dance and beat up several of them before he met Mulford Dorlon. Mulford, the father-in-law of Uncle Bud, was not a man to be trifled with, and he ended the fighting spree with one punch.

"Hit him under the jaw and broke his neck," reported Uncle Bud, and he swore to Rayford that the story was true.

By the end of the nineteenth century, all of that was simply part of the lore. The frontier had faded and the pirates were gone, and Bayou La Batre, as the town had come to be known, had developed a multilayered identity. It was, first of all, a fishing village where shellfish flourished in the labyrinth of bayous, as well as the waters of Mississippi Sound, that shallow and bountiful part of the Gulf that lay just north of Dauphin Island and extended all the way to New Orleans. But Bayou La Batre and next-door Coden had also entered their glory years of posh hotels and tree-shaded streets and tourists pouring in from all over the country. The Bay Shore Railroad, jutting south from Mobile, cut through the heart of the lush coastal forests and made it an easy trip for the visitors.

And then came the fateful storm of 1906.

It began on a Wednesday afternoon, September 26, the winds first blowing in from the north. That was a good sign. Whatever their force, the powerful gusts were working against the waves, that wall of water surging up from the south. But then the wind shifted and the water rushed ashore, flooding the downtown streets of Mobile and pounding the homes and hotels of the Bayou. Three days later, a Mobile writer, George B. Toulmin, paid a visit to the area.

"Those who escaped with their lives saved nothing," he wrote, "absolutely nothing, even the few clothes they had on being stripped and torn into threads and fragments."

A fishing boat returns to
port in Bayou La Batre.
© 1998 Sheila Hagler

Along the Gulf Coast, the death toll soared to 135, and many years later Arthur
McRoy, a Coden resident and part-time historian, still kept personal records of the
storm. His maternal grandfather, Yancey Pringle, then a captain in the Alabama
National Guard, came to the community in 1906 to direct the burial of the Bayou's
dead. He left a meticulous account of what he found: "Body of a white man about 20
or 22 years old . . . identification not possible. . . . Body of a white man heavy built
. . . had on a double breasted rubber coat."

Such was the legacy of 1906, and more storms followed in 1916 and 1925. One
by one, the hotels began to close, unable to withstand the devastation wrought by

the weather, and the inevitable evolution of the coastal economy. But the people survived, their subsistence, now more than ever, tied to the sea.

As their technology evolved in the twentieth century, the oystermen moved from hand tongs to mechanical dredges then back to the tongs when they discovered that the dredges were causing damage to the reefs. The shrimpers, meanwhile, were also working to perfect their technique. At the beginning of the century, they worked with cast nets, often going out alone in their bare wooden skiffs. The nets were usually braided by hand, then dyed with the bark of a red oak tree, which became a cottage industry in the town. But as the century progressed, so did the boats—their engines strong enough to pull trawling nets—and Arthur McRoy, among many others, recalls with nostalgia "the sound of the engine on a misty November morning."

Nostalgia aside, the catches steadily increased in volume, white shrimp and brown, depending on the territory and the season, and by the middle of the century the boats had also increased in size. These were steel-bottomed trawlers, many of them sixty-five feet in length, capable of handling the open waters of the Gulf. The Bayou's catch soon expanded to other species of shrimp, including pinks and royal reds from off the coast of Florida.

A shipbuilding industry sprang up as well, and Bayou La Batre became a prosperous, blue-collar town, filled with people who were proud of who they were—proud of their ancestors, and proud of the ethic that helped them survive. Marie Schjott was one of the old-timers who remembered how it was growing up. She was raised—and still lived as a grandmother well into her eighties—on the eastern bank of the largest and deepest of the local estuaries. Mrs. Schjott's land had been farmed by her grandfather Oliver Stillwell Cain in the nineteenth century, but it was already a legendary patch of ground. It was precisely the place where the spirited teenager Henriette Huet met and ran away with Jean-Baptiste Baudreau, and where their son, Pierre-Baptiste, took up residence in 1792.

The Cains bought the land in the nineteenth century and built a big white house in the shade of a towering live oak tree that was said to be seven hundred years old. The tree is still there, battered through the years by the waves of hurricanes, but still majestic and still standing proud.

"That tree was in our history books," says Marie's son Randy. "It was supposed to be the largest in the state of Alabama."

It was, at the least, a prized climbing tree for the generations of children growing up in the area, and it was one of the things that Marie missed most when her family moved to Mobile for several years. She was in the third grade at the time, and although she returned at the end of high school, it was, she says, a thirty-mile exile that nearly broke her heart.

"All that time, I grieved," she said. "I said as soon as I got back, they'd have to shoot me out with a cannon if I ever left again."

As a teenager, she remembered, she went to work in the family oyster shop, helping to unload the boats when they arrived at the dock, later prying open the thick, twisted shells, removing the delicate meat inside. She worked also at a local drugstore, giving shots to people who were sick. When the Depression hit in the 1930s, she would often take a boat to Dauphin Island, back before the bridge was built, and deliver medicine to the people over there. The five-mile trip could be dangerous at times, "but I never regretted it," said Mrs. Schjott. "I couldn't have slept if I didn't do it. Over here in our community, we were getting by. But times on the island were hard back then."

Such was the ethic she grew up with. You worked hard and pulled your own weight, but you kept an eye on neighbors in need, knowing that they would do the same for you. Her son Randy, who was raised the same way, was a shrimper for years and a part-time mechanic who occasionally wrote poems about the place he was raised. One of his favorites was a tribute written to past generations—"a time of wooden boats and iron men"—when a way of life took shape on the Bayou that has survived well into the twenty-first century.

By most accounts, it was a feeling that cut across ethnic lines. For much of its history, the white majority in Bayou La Batre has shared a set of values with the African Americans, and later the Asians, who lived nearby. The black minority was always small—in the year 2000, about 10 percent of the local population—but even in the days of racial segregation, when tension and hostility were often in the air, members of the African American community embodied the same sense of pride and self-reliance that characterized their neighbors.

Just a few miles west of Bayou La Batre, in the town of Grand Bay, the black community built their own school in 1919 with the help of a grant from Julius Rosenwald, president of Sears, Roebuck & Company. Rosenwald, a Jewish million-aire, was born during the presidency of Abraham Lincoln (just a few blocks, in fact, from Lincoln's birthplace in Illinois), and he had a special interest in the issue of race. "The horrors that are due to race prejudice come home to the Jew more forcefully than to others of the white race," he explained, "on account of the centu-ries of persecution which they have suffered."

In 1912, Rosenwald joined the board of trustees of Tuskegee Institute, and he became a friend of Tuskegee's president, Booker T. Washington. The two of them spent many hours talking about the state of education, and at Washington's urging, Rosenwald set out to build schools for African American children in the South. He built nearly five thousand before he was through, working most often with local black leaders, and the Grand Bay Elementary School for Colored was one of the first to open its doors. More than eighty years later, in 2007, the oldest living graduate of the school, Clinton M. Hayes, who was ninety-six, returned to the site with a small group of former students to dedicate a historical marker.

Such was the pride of the local black citizens.

Nancy McCall was raised with that spirit. In the 1950s, as an African American child in Coden, she listened to the stories her grandmother told about how her family came to be there. Many of them lived on a pitted dirt road called Midway Street, having arrived in the 1920s and '30s, most as refugees from Mississippi. They had worked the cotton fields not far from Waynesboro, a town just west of the Alabama line, where they confronted the cruelties of the sharecropping system. No matter how hard they worked, no matter how many hours they spent in the fields, they could never get ahead. At the end of the year, they always seemed to owe more than they had earned, and they knew that things would only get worse if they dared to challenge the plantation owners.

Sometime in the late 1920s, they began to hear stories of the Alabama coast, a place where a man who was willing to work could always manage to take care of his family. Crate West, Nancy McCall's great-uncle, decided that was where they should go, but he knew it was a move that carried some risk. In the part of Mississippi where he lived, the plantation owners, usually in league with the local police, kept close watch on the sharecropping families, restricting their movements and their ability to assemble or gather with their neighbors. West hated that way of life, regarding it as not much better than slavery, and he was grumbling about it one day in the fields when an old black man passed by on the road.

"You stay at this plantation?" the old man asked.

"Yeah," said West.

"Man, you stay at a bad place."

Coden community activist Nancy McCall, *right*, and church administrator Elizabeth Sigler pose on a Sunday morning at Sweet Bethel Baptist Church.

They kept on talking, and the old man, Bruce Russell, said he knew a way to get them out. He was part of an Underground Railroad of sorts, a twentieth-century throwback to the days of slavery when people grew desperate enough to run away. Russell said they should leave right away — that very night, in fact — and if they would meet him in the woods just after midnight, he would take them to a place where the freight train passed.

According to the story handed down in the family, Crate and the others packed biscuits, salt meat, and a half gallon of molasses, all of it carefully wrapped in a quilt, and they waited until the moon was straight overhead. They found Bruce Russell where he said he would be, and he led them to a place where the train slowed down on its run to Mobile.

"They jumped on board," says Nancy McCall, "and around daylight they were getting hungry. They unwrapped the food and discovered the top had popped off the molasses. They sopped biscuits and salt meat right off of that quilt."

A few years later, after the Wests and all their extended family had settled in the Bayou, Bruce Russell finally made the journey himself. He was pushing a hundred by that time, but he was still a large and powerful man, still a hard worker, everybody said, and they were happy to have him as part of the community. He worked for a time in other people's gardens — "had the sharpest ax and hoe you ever saw," says McCall — and when he died, he was buried behind Sweet Bethel Baptist Church, as one of the most honored men in his community.

Those were the days, says Elsie Simmons, another of West's descendants in the Bayou, when people worked long hours and were proud of what they did. Her own father, she says, worked for years in the "paperwood" business, cutting timber and hauling it away in a truck that he had paid for himself. "Not many blacks had trucks in those days," she says, and for her father it was a source of deep satisfaction. His business went well until a tree fell on him one day in the woods. No longer able to do heavy lifting, he went to work as a chauffeur for Dr. Mose Tapia, the town physician, and he also drove the local school bus.

Those were bittersweet days in Bayou La Batre, when segregation was still a fact of daily life. There had been a time, when Crate West and the others first came from Mississippi, that blacks who were working anywhere in the town knew they needed to be home before sundown. Things were better by the 1950s, especially, it seemed, along Midway Street, where black and white families lived side by side, their children playing and growing up together. And as Nancy McCall remembered it later, there was even an integrated baseball team.

Looking back on it, it seems clear now that those first cracks in the walls of segregation foreshadowed a kind of live-and-let-live acceptance that was stronger in the end than any residue of prejudice. That sense of acceptance was tested in the 1970s when the Asian refugees moved in, soon making up one-third of the community population. But after some inevitable tension early on, including racial slurs in the schools, life in the fishing village returned to a harmonious routine.

"It's a welcoming town," says Sakhoeum Khan, a seventeen-year-old Cambodian girl. "That is one of the things that I like."

Not that most residents are inclined to romanticize Bayou La Batre. On the contrary, they are the first to admit that the town has its flaws—an admission clearly borne out by the facts. By the closing years of the twentieth century, according to the U.S. Census, the community's average family income was less than twenty-five thousand dollars a year. Only 55 percent of the Bayou's residents had earned as much as a high school diploma, and fewer than 8 percent had a college degree. To complicate those unimpressive rankings, Bayou La Batre

and the communities around it are afflicted now by drug-related crime that has spread to the countryside from the cities.

In the predawn hours of March 29, 2007, law enforcement officials from five different agencies descended on a cluster of Bayou houses, rounding up twenty-seven people suspected of dealing crack cocaine. The suspects came from every corner of the spectrum—African American, Asian, and white—including an eighty-one-year-old grandmother. "I think this will send a message," said Bayou mayor Stan Wright, "that we are not going to tolerate this." But the message had been sent before, without success. There had been major raids in the same part of town, which is just up the street from Alba Middle School, in 1996 and again in 2001–2002. But the drug dealers always trickled back in.

The hands of Coden residents are busy cleaning fish after a successful day at sea.

Photo by Thea Whalen
© MOC 2006

Lazarus Johnson, an octogenarian living two blocks from the school, said in an interview in 2007 that he still saw the drug sales happening every day. Soon after the raid of March 29, he put up a warning sign in his yard, telling drug dealers they better stay away. "YOU WILL GO TO JAIL," he wrote.

For many of the old-timers, the specter of drugs was another sign of change—of something precious that was slowly being lost. Not that the olden days were idyllic. There had always been drunken brawls and fistfights and turf war scuffles between boys growing up in different neighborhoods. But it was, in the end, a good place to live, and Floyd Bosarge, among many others, did what he could to keep it that way.

Every Monday evening for as long as most of his neighbors could remember, Mr. Floyd, as he was known in the later years of his life, played host to a fish fry in the shed behind his house. This was also the place where he built his wooden boats, and nearly every Monday, as the mullet or the oysters sizzled in the fryer, some of the men would inspect his latest creation—a fishing-boat-in-the-making, the plywood carefully glued to the frame in a style that made his boats unmistakable. There was no alcohol at any of these occasions, just a handful of men, ranging in age from their thirties to their eighties, gathering once a week to swap stories.

Sometimes they drifted toward the realm of legend—like the time the oysterman Buddy Bosarge, who lived in a lean-to behind his mother's burned-out house, was tonging for oysters on West Fowl River. Buddy, it seems, had a wooden boat, equipped with a twenty-five-horsepower motor, and he could travel at a pretty good clip through the bayous. But on this day, an Indian came by in a one-man canoe and challenged Buddy to a race. To make it interesting, they both agreed that the winner would keep the other man's boat.

According to the story, Buddy Bosarge revved his engine and took off down the bayou, the Indian paddling his canoe alongside, slowly but surely pulling into the lead. "First thing you know, that Indian was gone," declared Chick Sprinkle, who was telling the story. "Buddy said, 'I lost my boat, my motor, and my oysters—everything I had—to that Indian.'"

Such stories inevitably produced a good laugh, but sometimes the conversation turned serious—when they talked, for example, about the pride the old-timers took in their work—how they always kept their oyster boats clean, and how some of the young people couldn't be bothered. In this treasure trove of Mr. Floyd's oral archives, they kept alive the values and memories of the Bayou, celebrating—without any premeditation or contrivance—an old and increasingly threatened way of life.

Floyd Bosarge, *left,* and his friend Edward Seward prepare the feast at a Monday night fish fry.
© 2007 Jerry Jones

At Floyd Bosarge's funeral in 2007, his great-nephew Camden Brown stands near a handmade boat filled with flowers.
© 2007 Sheila Hagler

And then in the winter of 2007, Floyd Bosarge died. He had already reached his eightieth birthday, and everybody knew that he didn't get cheated. But it was also hard to believe he was gone. Everywhere you looked, you saw his handmade boats in the rivers and the bays, and on the day of his funeral at Coden Bible Church, the last of those boats—a blue-bottomed skiff he had just finished building with his great-nephew—took its place on a trailer at the head of the procession.

They filled the boat with the flowers, then closed the casket, and carried Mr. Floyd—dressed as always in his fishing cap, jeans, and faded work shirt—in a slow and mournful procession to his grave.

2 *The Refugees*

When people start to talk about changes in the area, sometimes they will talk about the 1970s, when the Asian refugees first came to the town. Those were terrible days in Cambodia, Vietnam, and Laos. Even now, Heang Chhun remembers how he felt on April 17, 1975, when Phnom Penh, the capital of Cambodia, fell into the hands of the Khmer Rouge. For the first few hours he took heart from the tone of the radio reports. "They say Cambodia now belong to Cambodians. Not fight anymore."

But it didn't take long for the horror to begin. Looking back on it now from the safety of his home near Bayou La Batre, Chhun, a strapping man in his sixties, with jet-black hair and steady eyes, repeats the same words over and over: "Somehow I survive. Somehow I survive."

He had good reason to believe that he wouldn't. The Khmer Rouge Communists, led by the maniacal Pol Pot, began a massive restructuring of Cambodian society, resulting in the forced evacuation of major cities and, before it was over, the murder and torture of more than two million people. The targets of this massive genocide included nearly everybody from the middle class—teachers, doctors, artists, and soldiers—and Chhun had been in the Cambodian army. He had a brother who was Khmer Rouge. "He looked for me," remembers Chhun, "and when we found one another, all we could do was hug and cry. He said, 'If you stay here, maybe I am the one who kills you.'"

A Buddhist temple stands at the heart of a Cambodian
community just north of Bayou La Batre.

Photo by Cynthia Morng © MOC 2007

With a small group of fellow refugees, Chhun and his family set out for Thailand —a journey that would take him nineteen days and exact a horrifying price. Their flight began in Kampong Thom province, the part of central Cambodia where they had lived. For the first three days Chhun and the others kept moving north, battling their way through the brambles and thorns of the Cambodian jungle. A few of the people in the group gave up. They had no food, no shoes on their feet, and they decided finally to turn themselves in. The others kept going, but the following day, the Khmer Rouge forces were waiting in ambush. When they opened fire, six people with Chhun were killed on the spot, including his wife and daughter. A son and another daughter were captured, but Chhun himself managed to escape, carrying with him a younger son who was nine.

They kept pushing north without any food, coming finally to the town where Chhun was born. "I go to my father's house," he said. "I see my sister. She had no words except crying." A few hours later, two brothers and a cousin came to see him, all of them armed with AK-47s and all of them loyal to the Khmer Rouge. After a meal of rice and dried fish, they told him he and the boy couldn't stay. They would surely be killed and they would put the rest of the family in danger. They said their father, a prominent man and mayor of the town, had already been shot, and the surviving family members were looked upon with suspicion. But there was still the matter of Chhun's little son, too weak now to keep going after ten days of travel without any food.

There had been another child, Chhun's brother said, who had been abandoned at a Buddhist temple up the road, and the Khmer Rouge had allowed him to stay. "My brother said, 'I take kid to temple, maybe he survive.' I think my brother had good idea."

Leaving his last remaining child, Chhun set out again for Thailand, climbing the rugged mountainside trail that led to the border, until at last he came to the refugee camp. He had been there for four or five months, living in the primitive safety that it offered, when another refugee from his hometown arrived. "He told me, Khmer Rouge arrested my brother and sister."

His son, meanwhile, had simply been left to fend for himself, the other families in the area too terrified to help him. Finally, one day, he ate a poisonous snail. "In the morning," said Chhun, "he lay down and die. My boy ate the wrong kind of snail."

After coming to America and helping to establish a community of Cambodians near Bayou La Batre, Chhun received word in 1991 that a son and daughter, the ones captured in the Khmer Rouge ambush, had somehow survived. It was joyful news on Angkor Road, the little dirt lane where thirty Cambodian families now live, for this is a neighborhood defined in part by the specter of loss. Yang Yath, a Cambodian grandmother, now living in a house not far from Chhun's, recently recounted her husband's execution by the Khmer Rouge. After three of her sons were also killed, she said she gathered her daughters and together they walked to the border with Thailand—two days and two nights over rugged terrain.

Her Bayou neighbor, Kan Ly, had spent four years in a Khmer Rouge prison camp, before escaping in 1979 and making a twenty-six-day journey to Thailand. And so it is that having lost so much to the terrors of war, they have now sought to recapture what they can. At the heart of their eighty-six-acre community is a Buddhist temple, where a pair of monks, one from Cambodia, the other from Sri Lanka, work to keep the ancient religion alive. In most of the homes, Cambodian is still the language of choice, and even the children who are fluent in English—the language that all of them speak in school—often speak Cambodian with members of their family. The gardens are brimming with Cambodian squash, and in the fish ponds Cambodian lilies bloom on the water.

The Cambodians are not alone in wanting to hold on to their heritage. Just a few miles away, on the Bayou La Batre–Irvington Highway, another Buddhist temple,

The Ngam family, who escaped the terrors of war and narrowly survived
Hurricane Katrina, pose in front of their Bayou home.

this one Laotian, stands back from the road, not far from the site of a Baptist tent revival, featuring Christian karaoke on a Saturday night. And finally, in the heart of Bayou La Batre, a third Buddhist temple serves the Vietnamese, the largest Asian group in the area.

Many of the immigrants came to the Bayou with the help of Catholic Refugee Services, and by the year 2000, there were 770 Asians out of a total population of 2,313. For some white families these were numbers that didn't sit well at first. "We looked around and the Vietnamese were everywhere," complained the owner of a seafood company. "We thought they were going to rename it Bayou Nam." And even today, one shrimper declares, "The Asian people mostly keep to themselves. They are not good neighbors, not civic-minded people."

But thirty years after the first immigrants arrived, such views are clearly in the minority. Far more common is the view of Rodney Lyons, a seafood broker, who maintains that the Asian refugees breathed new life into the local economy. "It made Bayou La Batre even more of a seafood production town," he says. "The Asian workers would pick 100 to 120 pounds of crabmeat a day. They doubled the production of American pickers. It made the crab business grow. If they were shucking oysters, they sometimes worked twelve hours a day, and changed the whole complexion of oyster production. They shrimped also. They bought up old boats and worked hard and upgraded their boats. They were heavy producers, and people had to respect that."

Hugh McClellan, a Bayou historian and former ecologist with the U.S. Army Corps of Engineers, says that from the very beginning the Asian workers in the seafood shops had "an outstanding work ethic. They would stay as long as there was product to handle, and when they left, the place would be as clean as their kitchen."

The anecdotal evidence was soon overwhelming. In 1999, *Mobile Register* reporter Roy Hoffman spent a long workday with Khampou Phetsinorath, a Laotian refugee who had survived five years as a prisoner of the Pathet Lao. By the time he escaped

An oyster shucker
takes a break from
her labors.

(Overleaf)
Vietnamese children
hold hands on the
dock near the mouth
of Bayou La Batre as
they await the return
of their father's boat.

in 1979, slipping away in the bamboo forests while his Communist captors looked the other way, his wife and children had fled from the country, believing he was dead. But Khampou learned in a refugee camp that his family had made it safely to America, and he followed them to Bayou La Batre, where his wife, Bounyong, had found steady work in a seafood shop.

Khampou went to work in the shops as well, and nearly twenty years later he was supporting his family by working seventeen hours a day. He began at dawn picking crabs in St. Elmo, a neighboring town. For the first six hours, he cut the meat from the tough inner shells, chatting as he worked at a long metal table piled high with boiled crabs. He and the other Asians at the table worked with a quiet and steady rhythm, until sometime early in the afternoon when Khampou began the second part of his job. He set out on his daily trip to Louisiana, jamming the gears of a sea-food truck that would soon be filled with another load of crabs. It was always a long and tedious journey, across Mississippi to the town of Slidell, then on to Chalmette and Delacroix Island. Even in 1999, there were still, occasionally, the veiled insults from whites he did business with in Louisiana. But Khampou pushed ahead.

When his truck was finally loaded with crabs, he turned again toward Alabama, rumbling east along Interstate 10. He arrived at the seafood shop around 11 P.M., exhausted now as he left the truck for the night crew to unload.

Such stories are common around Bayou La Batre. Heang Chhun, now president of the Cambodian Association of Mobile, says the work is still hard for many refugees, what with long hours picking crabs, shucking oysters, and trawling for shrimp in the waters of the Gulf. But there is perspective also, and a curious peace, rooted in the terrible things they survived.

"Nothing is perfect," Chhun concludes. "We consider it okay."

Father Bieu Nguyen, a priest at St. Margaret's Catholic Church, has thought a lot about the immigrant experience. As a teenager, he was one of the boat people, those desperate Vietnamese refugees who fled the country after the fall of Saigon in 1975, and again in 1979, when fighting broke out between Communist Vietnam and its neighbors. Nguyen seldom talks about his own experiences, the threat of pirates and other perils at sea as he and others crowded onto small boats and headed out to international waters, hoping to be rescued by a freighter.

But as pastor now at one of the most important churches in the Bayou, he has listened to stories that others have told. He came to St. Margaret's in 2005 to help rebuild after Hurricane Katrina. He already knew the importance of the church, how it had been constructed on the eastern shore of the Bayou almost exactly a hundred years ago, and how its wooden dock with a statue of Jesus standing just behind it is home every year to the Blessing of the Fleet, the most important ceremony in the town. Once a year in May, thousands of people—black, white, Asian—gather on the grounds for a festive weekend of games, food, and selling local crafts. Finally, at the end of the day, the mood turns serious as Father Nguyen and Mobile's Archbishop Oscar Lipscomb, dressed in his white and purple robes, stand before the rows of decorated boats and offer their prayers for the safety of the fleet: "God bless your going out and your coming in; the Lord be with you at home and on the water."

After working in the Bayou and attending several of those celebrations, Nguyen says he has been struck less by the differences between ethnic groups than by their similarities in character. He notes that nearly everybody in his church, where a quarter of the congregation is Vietnamese, has experienced some kind of life-threatening upheaval, ranging from war to deadly hurricanes. "But these are strong, proud people," he says. "They are rebuilding, moving on with their lives."

It is true, of course, that like most immigrants in the history of the country, the Vietnamese had trouble at first. "There is always misunderstanding and friction," says Nguyen. "There are language barriers and cultural differences that can lead to suspicion, and with most of the immigrants, a part of their hearts is still back at home. But this is their new home. Their sons and daughters are much more Americanized. They speak fluent English; they live in the circumstances they are in. It gets better and better over time."

As Nguyen will acknowledge, there are still some families who struggle in the Bayou, who have worked as hard as anyone else, but find themselves dogged by tragedy and disappointment. Joey Nguyen, for example (no relation to the priest), was spending the summer of 2006 working in a liquor store near his home. He had just graduated from Alma Bryant High School, where a couple of teachers who worked with him closely saw him not only as promising and bright, but impressive in his skill with other people. He was a big, dark-haired kid with an easy smile, full of self-possession and confidence—a natural candidate for college. But Joey decided he had to put it off. His family, he said, needed him at home.

He had moved to Bayou La Batre as a child, a fourth-grader who came with his parents, four siblings, and two sets of cousins. His mother was Laotian, his father Vietnamese, a refugee couple who had met in Alabama and started a life together in this country. When they came to the Bayou, Joey's mother, Bong, immediately went to work in an oyster shop, prying open the shells and extracting the tender meat inside. His father, Phi Nguyen, became a shrimper, first as a crew member on ocean-going trawler that often spent weeks or even months out at sea. Finally, Phi Nguyen bought a boat of his own, and for the next five years he shrimped for himself. But then in 2005, he began to develop high blood pressure, and early on, there were warning signs of a stroke. But Mr. Nguyen kept pushing.

"He wanted to work," said Joey. "He cares about others more than himself."

The stroke, when it came, was a devastating blow, leaving Mr. Nguyen partially paralyzed and unable to speak, and leaving the family with financial problems. Joey, until then, had planned to go to college, hoping eventually to become a radiologist,

A Buddhist temple serving the Vietnamese community survived Hurricane Katrina not far from the waterfront in Coden.

Photo by Mui Lam © MOC 2007

but those dreams had to go on hold for a while. He went to work at the liquor store, and then at a shipyard over in Mobile, doing what he could to help support his family. When he felt disappointed, or even resentful, he said he just thought about his father—his hard work and sacrifice for his family.

"I want to be more like him," said Joey.

He knew there were others who had it just as bad—troubled families where the parents had divorced or the father drank himself into a stupor every day. But there were some young Asians who had managed to build on their parents' hard work, excelling in high school and going off to college, where they studied for new and promising careers. Christy Te, for example, was a young Cambodian who won a full scholarship to Vanderbilt. She graduated high in her class, and while she was waiting to enter law school, she decided to return to Bayou La Batre and go to work for Boat People S.O.S. It was an activist organization that helped Bayou families, especially the Asians, rebuild their lives after major hurricanes, and also offered other family services from language tutoring to breast cancer screening. Christy wanted to give something back, and Boat People seemed like a good opportunity.

She chose to work as a tutor. She remembered her days at Alma Bryant High School, where she had seen how some of her Asian peers struggled, becoming pregnant, mired in gang life, or trapped in a cycle of dead-end work in order to help their own families survive. Even Christy's older siblings had gone to work in the seafood shops—long hours shucking oysters or picking crabs—and couldn't concentrate as much on school.

"I feel lucky," she said. "I don't take it lightly. A lot of refugee kids don't make it to college."

For those in Bayou La Batre that do, there are the competing pulls of the outside world—and all the opportunity it offers—and a deeply felt sense of family and place. "Home really grounds me," said Christy Te.

Tran Nguyen understood that feeling. In 2007, she graduated from the University of South Alabama and accepted a teaching job in Texas. But in the weeks leading up to her departure, she held to the rhythms of Bayou La Batre, arriving with her mother around 3 A.M. for a day of picking crabs at Drawdy's seafood shop. By the time she would take her place on the stool, the night shift had already boiled the load of live crabs, brought in the night before from Louisiana, and removed the outer shells, before separating the crab bodies from the claws. Tran's specialty, she said, is cleaning the claws, while her mother prefers to cut the meat from the bodies.

Most mornings they will have made a good start by four, and the crab shop is usually buzzing with three different languages—English, Cambodian, and Vietnamese—punctuated often by the sound of laughter. The Vietnamese workers tend to sit together, as do the Cambodians and the African Americans, all of them suffused by the pungent odor of the crabs, a stench so familiar that they take it for granted. They are paid by the pound, $1.50 to $2.00, depending on what kind of crabmeat it is, and on an average day Tran can take home $100 or more. That is part of the reason she does it; the pay is decent, her boss Terry Drawdy treats her with respect, and her hours are as flexible as she wants to make them.

But there is something else about the crab shop. For Tran and her family, it's a tradition they've shared since 1991 when they emigrated here from Vietnam and finally found safety and freedom on the Bayou.

Twenty years earlier, back during the war, her father Truat Nguyen was an officer in the South Vietnamese Air Force. But then came the day, April 30, 1975, when Saigon fell to the Communist forces, and the last Americans withdrew from the country. The South Vietnamese were left to their fate, and Truat Nguyen was one of thousands taken away to labor camps, where he managed to survive for five and a half years.

Sometimes even now, the family will gather together in the evenings, and Mr. Nguyen will tell the story of those times. "Sometimes my daughter asks me," he says. "What I tell her is what I know."

A slight, gentle man with a ready smile, he will talk about all the things he survived—about his bombing missions in the Vietnamese Air Force and, as he understood it, the struggle for freedom against invaders from North Vietnam. And he will talk about his years in the camps. "We knew the day we went in," he says. "We did not know the day we get out. For some it might be three years, for others six, some maybe eighteen. We work hard every day in the camps, some in the jungles, some along the sea or the rivers. We cut trees, perhaps dig new canals. They wanted us to work and work and get less food. They kill us day by day. Mostly, we lost our minds. Everybody thinks only about getting food—think about nothing else."

When he was finally released in 1980 and reunited with his family, he waited ten years before leaving the country. He operated a bicycle taxi—pedaling through the streets of Tayninh, offering people rides on his two-seater bike—and if the work was demeaning for an educated man, he now says he wants to keep the memory alive. Partly, he thinks, his children and grandchildren need to know how it was. But in the end, he says, his is also a story of hope, for he came to America and was able to make a living for his family—first in the seafood shops of the Bayou, where he worked along-side his wife Nhung Nguyen, and later as a truck driver for the city of Mobile.

"Right here," he says, "I have freedom. I have human rights. But we are here not only for the parents. We are here for the children to have a better life."

In the end, perhaps, the most striking thing about the refugees' stories is their basic similarity to those told by others in the history of the Bayou. Even in the time of Joseph Bosarge, when he applied for his original land grant, caught in a moment of poverty and shame, he came to a place where he could build a better life. The same was true of the black refugees who came on the eve of the Great Depression, some of them running from the last remnants of slavery, catching a freight train down from Mississippi because they had heard you could find steady work. They found it, of course, and so did the Asians, and the flip side was that as the twentieth century gave way to the twenty-first, all of the people of Bayou La Batre—white, black, and Asian—faced a new set of challenges very different from those of the past.

No longer, it seemed, were a little bit of luck and a sturdy work ethic all it took to get along. In the brave new world of a global economy, there were changes in the seafood industry itself—an $80 million enterprise in the Bayou, which represented 85 percent of the area's economy. Perhaps most urgently, higher fuel prices and competition from imported shrimp, now cheaper than those caught closer to home, were squeezing the profit margins for the shrimpers. "It's been just devastating," said Robert Shipp, chair of marine sciences at the University of South Alabama. "The future of the shrimp industry is not good at all." Crabs and oysters have been more stable, but in Bayou La Batre, shrimp production has been the biggest industry, and to complicate matters, there has been an ongoing conflict between the shrimping fleet and commercial sports fishermen in pursuit of red snapper. The snapper are often caught in the shrimp nets, a problem that has led, over time, to an intricate set of environmental regulations. The oystermen, too, have been embroiled in environmental debates. Mechanical dredging has recently been legalized again, and many oystermen fear that despite the efficiency of the dredging process, it will do major damage to the oyster beds.

Such was the atmosphere of economic insecurity when Alabama developer Tim James announced a plan in 2005—some four months before Hurricane Katrina—to build condominiums along the Bayou waterfront. He put forth a $200 million proposal, the heart of which included the purchase of Lightning Point, a spit of land where the bayou empties into Mississippi Sound. There, James proposed building high-rise condominiums with a commanding view of that part of the Gulf. Some in Bayou La Batre were excited, seeing the potential for economic progress. Others, particularly the owners of smaller businesses, feared they would simply be swept aside. Along other parts of the Alabama coast, they had seen how a trend toward gentrification and sprawling high-rises could threaten the fundamental character of the area. They feared the same for Bayou La Batre.

And then in the summer of 2005, as those feelings of uncertainty were nearly at their peak, the hurricane of the century came surging through the Gulf. It was a terrifying moment in the history of the town.

3 *Katrina*

On August 23, 2005, Tropical Depression 12 formed near the southeastern tip of the Bahamas. The following morning, it was officially upgraded to a tropical storm and given the name Katrina as it moved northwest through the warm waters of the Atlantic Ocean. Two hours before making landfall in Florida, Katrina finally became a hurricane — a Category 1 — and even though Florida had seen far worse, weather forecasters were already worried. They knew Katrina had the momentum to sweep across the southern tip of the state and emerge again in the Gulf of Mexico, where the water temperature was eighty-five degrees. It was, as one historian later noted, the "perfect incubator" for a catastrophic storm.

On Saturday morning, August 27, Katrina continued to churn through the Gulf, drifting west and gaining steadily in size and strength. By the following morning, it had reached the status of a Category 5 with winds of 175 miles per hour, and even though it would weaken slightly before hitting land, it had already stirred a massive wall of water that was moving toward the coast. At 6:10 on the morning of August 29, both the wind and the water hit the shores of eastern Louisiana, and though Katrina was now a Category 3, with winds of 120 miles per hour, the storm surge was one of the worst on record.

The national media focused — quite understandably — on the death and devastation in the city of New Orleans, with some additional attention to Mississippi,

An oyster boat makes its way slowly up Bayou Coden, as life moves on after Hurricane Katrina.

where the coastal towns of Waveland and Bay St. Louis were nearly wiped away. But the terror extended to Bayou La Batre, where the winds came ashore with hurricane force and the storm surge grew to nearly fifteen feet.

Loan Vo remembers how it was. A child of eleven, she lived in the Bayou in a part of town called Little Saigon, which was only a couple of feet above sea level. As the water continued to rise on August 29, the family saw quickly that their house was going to flood. They packed what they could into their van and drove a quarter of a mile to Shambeau's grocery, a flat brick building on slightly higher ground. Loan, a dark-haired girl with soft, gentle eyes, huddled in the van with the members of her family—her brother, her sister, her parents, and their dog. There in the driving wind and rain, with the temperature rising inside the car, they watched as the water kept getting deeper.

"We couldn't believe our eyes," remembered Loan, "and the water kept coming."

Finally, her father decided to go back, for the family had left something precious at the house. "In our custom," said Loan, "when people die, we keep their picture. We had one of my great-grandma and one of my great-grandpa. My father decided to go back and get them, and we were very scared. The water was deep and he had to swim." At one point, she said, Hung Nguyen was forced to dive beneath the waves to escape a flying rooftop that had blown off a house. But he found the photographs and put them safely in a plastic bag; and though it seemed like hours before he returned, he managed to save the two family treasures.

Just a few hundred yards to the west, Mary Wilkerson, another Bayou resident, peered out at the storm from the cabin of a shrimp boat, a sturdy trawler that was tied near the dock of St. Margaret's Church. Her family had already lived through unspeakable tragedy, having lost a son in an accident and a daughter in a murder, and now they were probably going to lose their home. They lived in a low-lying area near Coden beach, and knowing that the flood was sure to overtake them, they decided to take their chances on the boat. Mrs. Wilkerson had brought her video camera, and she carefully recorded the fury of the storm, measuring the steady rise of the water by the statue of Christ that stood near the dock. The surge first covered the chiseled hem of his robes, then rose to his waist, and finally there was no sign of Jesus at all.

Just up the street from the church, a young Bayou couple, who did not want their name to be used, measured the surge in a more elemental way. As the water kept rising inside their house, they climbed to the top of the kitchen cabinets, and as they huddled in a space just below the ceiling, they prayed that the flood would somehow recede.

Listening later to those kinds of stories, Nancy McCall flashed back to an earlier time. Again and again growing up in Coden, she had heard the old-timers talk about the storm of 1906 and the indelible imprint it had left in its wake. Her pastor, Will Prichard, used to preach about it on Sundays, telling the story more than once from the pulpit about how the Lord had come to him in a dream. It was still a few months before the storm, and God told the preacher he needed to move. Reverend Prichard obeyed, and when the hurricane hit, it washed away the house he had been living in. But the worst part was the fact that there were others who apparently didn't get the warning, and the image that stayed with Prichard through the years was of mothers and babies in the tops of pine trees. Some were alive, clinging to the limbs that saved them from the flood, while others had drowned, their bodies wedged between the branches by the water.

"He would cry, even in the pulpit, when he told that story," said Nancy McCall. "He never could get that picture from his mind."

McCall suspected there would be the same aftershock from Katrina, for in her own lifetime of dealing with storms, she had never seen anything that approached it. And for the most part, neither had the country. Historian Lawrence Powell of Tulane University argued in an article in 2007 that Katrina was one of those watershed events that shifted the basic perceptions of the nation. For the better part of a week, television crews had recorded the disaster—how in the devastated heart of New Orleans, people still huddled together on rooftops, or waded chest-deep through the muck of flooded streets, or crowded the convention center and the Superdome, pleading for medical help that didn't come. And there above it all in Air Force One, two days after the storm had passed, was President George W. Bush, peering helplessly from the window of his cabin and speculating to one of his aides that things were probably even worse on the ground.

The president's poll numbers began spiraling downward, even as the Katrina death toll was rising, but the greatest villain in the hurricane disaster—the poster child for governmental incompetence—became the Federal Emergency Management Agency (FEMA). The first FEMA convoy into New Orleans managed to get lost and wound up instead at the Sam's Club in Metairie. The agency turned down an offer of resources—three hundred boats, eleven aircraft and four hundred law enforcement officers—from the U.S. Department of the Interior. And the agency's director, Michael Brown, responded with what appeared to be indifference as other offers of assistance poured in—from Amtrak to Home Depot, from the government of Cuba to the government of Kuwait, from the state of Florida to the University of North Carolina.

As historian Douglas Brinkley later wrote, "Brown delayed the deployment of all such offers of aid, insisting that they wait until a chain of command could be established." Indeed, at one point FEMA even threatened to arrest people taking airboats into New Orleans—to assist in the rescue of those still stranded—without proper authorization from the agency.

Nor were the problems confined to New Orleans. In Bayou La Batre, FEMA had delivered, two months after the storm had passed, fewer than half of the travel trailers it had promised. The waters of Katrina had flooded most of the homes in the Bayou, as well as those in neighboring Coden, leaving more than five hundred families without a place to live. Some people had simply been forced to leave, while others were in tents or crowded in with relatives, and some, like the family of Amber Hill, decided to return to their storm-damaged houses.

As a high school freshman, Amber wrote a paper about her experience: "There was no running water, no gas, no power, and no way of keeping cool. Smothering from the heat, I was forced to sleep sweaty and in nothing but a bathing suit. My parents and I could not bathe and had nothing to eat. We nearly starved . . . but food wasn't our only concern. We had no place to call home anymore. Instead, we were forced to sleep in our old home where mold had begun to grow on the walls. Towards the end of the second week, I couldn't hold back the tears."

Later, after life had begun to stabilize, Amber thought hard about her hurricane experience and the contrast with other parts of her life—to the days, for example, when she was a little girl, and her great-grandparents would take her for rides along Coden beach. "We would drive around the beach before church every Sunday," she remembered. "We would look out at the ocean in the morning sunlight because they wanted us to see the full beauty of life. I didn't understand it until recently, but they were right. There is so much beauty in the world. Sometimes we need to stop and take it in."

For Amber and others, that kind of perspective was a part of their culture, as natural as air, and it would become a foundation for their recovery from the storm. But they also knew it would be a hard climb. For one thing, the seafood economy was now in shambles. Some thirty-two shrimp boats docked in the Bayou had been ripped from their moorings and stranded in the marsh, and FEMA had refused to

A Coden family stands before the wreckage of their home after Hurricane Katrina.

Photo by Adrian Overstreet © MOC 2005

help get them back. On November 22, 2005, FEMA officials announced they would pay to remove only three boats, because they posed a health threat to nearby houses. The owners of the other twenty-nine trawlers would have to pay for the removal themselves, or pay FEMA to do it—at a cost of sixty thousand dollars per vessel.

"It's awful," said Bayou La Batre mayor Stan Wright.

The *Mobile Register* called it "shameful" and mocked the "sensitivity" of FEMA coordinator Mike Bolch, who declared: "These vessel owners should have had insurance." As the *Register* noted, the U.S. Coast Guard, which had performed superbly throughout the disaster, had hired a contractor to remove the boats, but FEMA stepped in to halt the operation. The agency proclaimed that the shrimp boat owners—working-class families on the edge of ruin—would have to reimburse FEMA for the salvage operation, and not the other way around. "Why are we not surprised?" asked the *Register's* editorial board.

Ultimately, the shrimp boat saga would have a happy ending, thanks to the intervention of two former presidents and the governor of Alabama. Since September, Bill Clinton and George H. W. Bush had been working together to raise money for Katrina relief, and it had proved to be an effective partnership—two men from different political parties, whose presidential race in 1992 had seen its share of bitter debate, now coming together with good humor and grace, seeking to accomplish something worthwhile. Both presidents had been to the Alabama coast—Bush to Dauphin Island, Clinton to Bayou La Batre, where he met with Mayor Wright and members of the community and promised to do whatever he could. Alabama governor Bob Riley, also exasperated with FEMA, promised to salvage the shrimp boats, whatever it took, and suggested that the Bush-Clinton money could be spent for that purpose.

The two presidents agreed, and the result was a successful, $1.4 million operation that began in July of 2006 and ended on September 23. The last boat recovered was the eighty-foot *Rip Tide*, a dark-bottomed trawler with an American flag flying near the mast. "The Bayou still has a long way to go," said city building inspector Tommy Reynoso, as the *Rip Tide* bobbed in the water near the dock. "But at least this chapter is closed."

During those early days of fighting back, it wasn't just presidents who came to offer hope. In the days and weeks just after the storm, help poured in from every corner of the country. "So many people came to our aid," Barbara Reid, a local Coden activist, wrote in an essay, "friends and strangers alike. These individuals sent food, water, cleaning supplies, monetary gifts and helping hands. Our survival was made possible through the unselfish acts of love. . . . It was the message of caring behind the material goods which has given us cause to continue."

Grace Scire was one of the early volunteers. She had recently moved to Alabama from Connecticut, buying a home with her husband on Mobile Bay. An attorney by training, she was looking forward to semiretirement and getting away from the New England cold. But then came Katrina. Having escaped the worst of the catastrophe themselves, she and her husband Jann drove down to the Bayou to see if there was anything they could do. Going door to door through the storm-ravaged streets, they found Asian families huddled together in mold-infested houses, isolated by the language barriers that were still a part of Bayou life. They also discovered that there was not enough medicine for people who were sick, regardless of their race, and Scire began making the rounds to the doctors' offices in neighboring Mobile, asking for pharmaceutical samples.

"They were happy to help," she said.

Throughout those days just after the storm, she was impressed by the massive outpouring from individuals and charitable organizations, and though there were turf battles and the inevitable competition for the same resources, there were people who worked heroically to help. But perhaps the thing that impressed her the most was the dogged resiliency of the community itself. "The people of the Bayou helping each other was amazing," she said. "They set up a shelter at the senior center and operated it themselves." There were people and cots filling up the gym floor, and during the day there were sandwiches and hot coffee and bottled water, and hot meals at night, and there was a medical clinic set up on the stage.

The clinic, especially, caught her attention, and the more Grace learned about the doctor in charge, the more astonished she was by the story. Dr. Regina Benjamin, she discovered, had been in the Bayou for nearly twenty years, operating a family practice clinic in the heart of the town. She was a throwback to the old-time physicians like Dr. Mose Tapia, who served the people of the Bayou La Batre from the 1920s to the 1960s—in the days when doctors still made house calls. Working at the turn of the twenty-first century, Benjamin, who would become U.S. Surgeon General in 2009, saw no reason why she shouldn't make house calls as well. She would leave her office, which was directly across the street from where Tapia's had been, and rumble through the town in her Toyota truck, dropping in on patients who couldn't come to her. Sometimes she would travel alone; other times she worked with Nell Bosarge Stoddard, her longtime nurse who was still going strong at the age of seventy-seven. Like the majority of people in Bayou La Batre, Nell Stoddard was white. Regina Benjamin was African American, but nobody paid much attention to that.

"She loves this community," said Stoddard. "She's very down-to-earth. There's nothing about her that puts people off."

Born in 1956, Benjamin grew up on the Alabama coast, just across the Bay in the little town of Daphne. There were family stories on which she was raised—how her grandmother, a matriarch in the black community of Daphne, would put out lemonade and sandwiches for the hoboes passing by on the highway. Perhaps Benjamin

Family physician Regina Benjamin poses in the cramped office of her clinic, which was destroyed by Hurricane Katrina.

© The Mobile Register

drew inspiration from that, but whatever the source, she had the same caregiver's mind-set. After graduating from Xavier University in New Orleans, she entered the Morehouse School of Medicine and later earned her degree from the University of Alabama–Birmingham.

She came to Bayou La Batre in 1987, a round-faced woman with a cheerful smile, and she quickly developed a deep affection for the place. "It was a lot like Daphne," Benjamin explains. "The patients here come from all walks of life, all different ethnic groups and cultures. They are warm-hearted people and there is no pretense. They love you or they hate you." She opened an office on Shell Belt Road, flanked by the retail shops of the town, but in 1998 the building flooded during Hurricane Georges, and she decided to move to higher ground. Her practice grew steadily on Tapia Street, but on the morning of Hurricane Katrina, the flood waters surged to her office and beyond.

In a *Reader's Digest* profile—one of many articles about her work—writer Lynn Rosellini offered this account of the damage: "All along the bayou, shrimp boats lay tossed onto dry land, masts and rigging tangled in tree branches. Crumpled piles of lumber marked where homes had stood, and a wash of slime inches deep seeped from the open doors of shops and restaurants. Benjamin pulled up to her medical clinic. The tidy gray building looked unscathed. But when she opened the door, the stench was almost enough to make her sit down. Seawater, old fish and dead crabs mingled with the raw sewage. Chairs and tables were tossed about as if they had been in a washing machine."

Nell Stoddard was there at Benjamin's side. "Oh my goodness," she said. "Here we go again."

The two of them waded into the muck and did their best to salvage what they could. But with the office in ruins, they set up makeshift quarters at the shelter, seeing patients on the stage. Throughout her time in Bayou La Batre, Benjamin had insisted on treating everyone—even those with no insurance and no ability to pay. "These people are very proud and don't accept handouts," she told an interviewer. "But times are very hard in the Bayou, and for some the most they can send me is five dollars a month." Everything was worse in the wake of the storm, and on many occasions Grace Scire saw the doctor write out a prescription and add a cryptic note to the pharmacist: "Bill me. Regina Benjamin."

"She said, 'I knew I could pay for it somehow,'" remembered Scire. "She said she could work extra shifts in an emergency room, or whatever it took."

There was also the matter of rebuilding the clinic. After months of work and hundreds of man-hours, it was set to reopen on January 2, 2006, when, incredibly, a fire broke out the night before and destroyed everything. The building carried a mortgage of $170,000, and in order to pay for rebuilding, Benjamin had mortgaged her own home for $210,000 and maxed out her credit cards for another $60,000. She had applied for grants to cover her pharmaceutical bills, and though at the moment she was drowning in debt, she stared at the charred remains of her clinic and turned to a reporter from the *Mobile Register*.

"We'll rebuild it," she said. "This will give me an opportunity to try and maybe do it differently. While I like what we had, maybe I can do it better."

Benjamin did, in fact, rebuild again, and by that time the people of the Bayou were well into the second stage of their recovery. The first stage had simply been a matter of survival—people searching through the wreckage and saving what they could, and spending their nights on cots at the shelter, or sleeping in tents, or maybe camping out in mold-infested homes. The good news was that they were not alone. From Volunteers of America to Catholic Social Services, at least eighty-two organizations were involved in a massive relief undertaking, and it fell to Mike Dillaber of Volunteer Mobile to try to pull all of those efforts together.

Dillaber came to the Bayou when the winds were still blowing at tropical storm force, and even on the outskirts of town he could see immediately that this was a bad one. Water, essentially, had engulfed the whole town, and almost everything in it was damaged. The first few hours were search and rescue—"pulling people out," as Dillaber put it—and then police and rescue workers set about bringing order from the chaos. Several hurricanes earlier, Volunteer Mobile, a private, nonprofit agency, had been designated by Mobile County to coordinate recovery from natural disasters, with Dillaber as point man.

In the case of Katrina, he immediately called in the most experienced organizations in the field—Mennonite Disaster Services, Lutheran Disaster Response, and the Methodist Disaster Recovery Ministry—and within a few hours many others followed, from smaller church groups to the Red Cross and the Salvation Army. The top priorities were obvious—setting up distribution sites for water and food, pulling trees off houses, clearing driveways, and assessing the overall damage. The more complicated issue was what to do next.

It had been ninety-nine years since the Bayou had seen anything like Katrina, and the storm of 1906 was more legend than memory. But now they were faced with a sobering truth. In a time of global warming, with mighty hurricanes more and more the norm, there were unanswered questions about how to rebuild. For Bayou La Batre as well as Coden, part of the identity, not to mention the charm, lay in their old-fashioned fishing-village feel—the houses clustered not far from the water, modest wood dwellings where people knew their neighbors, and where rent and house payments were still within reason.

But in many ways, it made no sense to simply build the neighborhoods back as they had been, for what would happen when the next storm came? Should the houses be elevated, and if so, by how much, and how could a shrimping family afford to do it?

These were the questions to be wrestled with, but before that, Mike Dillaber and the army of volunteers began doing "tear-outs." They removed the mud-soaked carpets from the houses, and the damaged drywall (the entire wall if the waterline had risen to more than four feet), knowing that those things had to be done. As their work continued, Regina Benjamin, among others, traveled to Thailand, studying that country's recovery from the catastrophic tsunami of 2004. One primary lesson she brought back to the Bayou was one that Dillaber already knew—the need to coordinate all the volunteers, to make sure that organizations talked to one another. In the following months, they were pleased by the way they were able to do that, as case managers helped local families sort through unfamiliar terrain—dealing with insurance, applying for FEMA grants to rebuild, and moving forward on the difficult road to recovery.

By a number of measures the progress was good, and within a few months, federal dollars were pouring into the Bayou. There was a $10 million grant from HUD to construct new housing north of downtown, more than a hundred affordably priced homes with mortgage assistance for families in need. There was a $1.3 million grant from the Bush-Clinton Fund to rescue the shrimp boats stranded on land, and there were millions more in federal dollars for roads and other infrastructure, including $24 million for a new sewer plant.

But it didn't take long before a bitter controversy was brewing, involving most notably the people of Coden. Nancy McCall, a community leader on Midway Street, said she and others from Coden's black community had bounced back and forth between the Mennonites, the Lutherans, and other relief agencies, and rarely got the help they were seeking. More than fourteen months after the storm, Barbara Reid, a Coden activist and leader of the South Bay Communities Alliance, led a delegation

A statue of the
Virgin Mary stands
incongruously on
the front porch of a
condemned house
in Little Saigon,
a Vietnamese
neighborhood in
Bayou La Batre.
© 2006 Sheila Hagler

to the county commission to complain about neglect of her area on the part of both government and relief agencies. Among other things, she told the commissioners, tons of debris piled up since Katrina had never been hauled away to the landfill.

Some Coden residents insisted that Mayor Stan Wright of Bayou La Batre had deliberately steered relief workers away from their community. And regardless of intent, another of the residents, Ernestine Williams, argued that the bottom line was indisputable: "We as Coden never got anything."

Certainly, it was true that Coden, an unincorporated community, was at a stark disadvantage in the pursuit of federal money. But in Coden, the charges of official and deliberate neglect only grew angrier over time—a disturbing reminder that those on the road to recovery from Hurricane Katrina would face more than their share of heartbreak and rage.

4 *The Long Road Back*

Peggy Denniston could see the pain in their eyes, these students of hers from Alba Middle School, and she was happy the day the principal came and told her they were going to embark on a project. It was only a few days after the hurricane. School had just reopened, and the campus cleanup was not yet complete. But she knew the students were happy to be back, for the school was an important part of their lives, a cornerstone of the community, in fact, and had been since 1918, when Peter F. Alba donated the land.

Alba was an impressive character in the Bayou. Born in 1833, he was a former Indian fighter and Confederate war veteran who came to Coden when the Civil War was over, and built an estate overlooking the water. He had a long white beard and piercing eyes, not a man to be trifled with, and in his later years, his passion was philanthropy. He was a founder of the Mobile Humane Society and a strong supporter of public education. In addition to giving land for the school in the Bayou, Alba was concerned about the neglect of black children. Although he lived in an era of rigid segregation, he donated property just down the coast for the Grand Bay Elementary School for Colored.

Such was his gentle impact on his place.

By the Great Depression, the Bayou school that bears Alba's name had come to a position of community prominence under the spirited leadership of Alma Bryant, who served as principal for thirty-seven years. "Miss Alma," as everybody called her, was a beloved figure, according to most accounts, but one of her students, Bun Stork, added a slightly different testimonial: "She would whip your butt," he acknowledged from experience. But most reminiscences took a serious tone, almost reverential, as people then and later reflected on Miss Alma's role in the Bayou.

"She marshaled the town's strength to withstand the Depression, various hurricanes and other disasters," concluded local writer Hope Bosarge, "by instilling in the community's youth a feeling that with sorrow comes joy, that no obstruction is so large that it cannot be overcome, and that, above all, to be proud of their heritage."

For Peggy Denniston and her fellow teachers at Alba, those kinds of lessons still seemed to apply in the days just after Hurricane Katrina. And when the principal of the school, James Gill, came by to say that the superintendent's office wanted photography students to document the storm, Denniston was elated by the possibilities. Over the next several weeks, she watched them work—students such as Adrian Overstreet, a beautiful girl with long red hair and uncommon poise, who traveled the Bayou roads with her mother, taking one picture of a three-sided house, the owner gazing out from where the other wall had stood before the water had torn it away. But Adrian's favorite, the one that best captured the reality of it all, was a picture that she called "Dazed and Homeless"—a Coden family and a little white dog standing in front of a pile of their belongings.

Later, in an interview with CNN, Adrian would describe her feelings this way: "The family is standing in front of a big old pile, like shoulder-high, and the dog is looking at you too. That one just jumped out at me. It's just so sad, and it really told the story—their house was standing right behind them . . . in little pieces."

Again and again, Denniston said, she found herself amazed at the power of the work. Saphea Khan snapped a picture of her little brother pointing to the waterline

Sophin Khan points to the waterline inside his family's home after Hurricane Katrina.
The flood stopped just below a painting of the Kahns' Cambodian homeland.

Photo by Saphea Khan © MOC 2005

in their house. Head-high to a child, the deluge had risen to a point just below the family's painting of Cambodia—a reminder of home and of losses suffered in a very different time. Jada Davis, who was then fourteen, took a photograph she called "Former Neighbor," the pilings of a house that had simply disappeared. Adam Rogers added "Can't Let Go," an old woman in a rocker in her storm-ravaged house, and Mui Lam shot a self-portrait in her empty dining room, right after new drywall had been installed.

"This shouldn't bring anybody down," Mui said. "It's just nature. Things happen. You just save it as a memory, and to show people in the future what you've been through."

In the end, the students' work became *Eyes of the Storm*, a traveling exhibition of photography and poetry that appeared in six different cities nationwide. In Bayou La Batre and the surrounding communities, people were proud of what the students had done, and the young people themselves talked often about their feelings of accomplishment. But it was also true that throughout the community, the grief kept coming at people in waves. Many months after the storm, in early March of 2007, a large bulldozer with its oversized claw ripped down the buildings on Shell Belt Road, the historic commercial district of the town. The area had stood like a ghost town for months, its storefronts damaged beyond all repair, but when the day finally came to pull them down, there were people who had to choke back tears.

"I look at these buildings being torn down," said Nell Bosarge Stoddard, the veteran nurse in Dr. Regina Benjamin's office. "It's heartbreaking when you see people's memories on the side of the road, stacked up and waiting to be taken to the dump."

In addition to the specter of material loss, and all of the history that went along with it, there had also been the loss of human life. According to the official statistics, none of the more than 1,800 people who were killed by Katrina in 2005 had actually died in Bayou La Batre—a welcome contrast to the catastrophic storm of 1906. But those statistics didn't tell the whole story, for there were a number of shrimpers in the Bayou area who tried to take their boats to safer ports, only to have the storm overtake them. One of those men, Charles Davis Nelson, who was still in his teens, never made it back home.

"He didn't survive," wrote his cousin Jana Jowers, in a paper she handed in at her school. "For my aunt, it was the end of the world."

And finally, there was the tragedy of Jada Davis, who had been an eighth-grader when Katrina hit and proved to be, in the weeks after that, a talented young artist in *Eyes of the Storm*—one of the natural leaders of the project. But on September 21, 2006, as she was entering her freshman year in high school, she was killed by a passing car as she was walking toward her school bus stop one morning. To her teachers and friends, it seemed for a while if the terrible news would never stop.

Grace Scire saw these things, and marveled at the resiliency of the people, at their stubborn ability to keep pushing ahead. After coming to the Bayou as a volunteer and doing what she could just after the storm, Scire had taken a job with Dr. Benjamin as chief operations officer of the clinic. They had raised the money to rebuild and expand, including more than $1 million in federal funding, channeled through Volunteers of America. By the early summer of 2007, Grace was proud of how the clinic had grown. They now had a physician's assistant and two more nurses in addition to Nell Stoddard, and there were medical students coming from the Morehouse School of Medicine. They had embarked on a new cancer-screening program, working with Boat People S.O.S. and the University of South Alabama, and they were hoping to hire at least two more doctors.

All of this represented real progress, but in the back of her mind, as Scire thought more broadly about the community, she could still feel an undertow of dread. What if another storm hit the Bayou? There were at least forty-nine families still in FEMA trailers, and in parts of Coden the situation was worse — people moving into rusted-out buses, surviving day to day in whatever primitive shelter they could find. And right behind her own doctor's office, squarely in the heart of Bayou La Batre, there was a row of mobile homes, many of them badly damaged already, the residents too poor to afford something new.

One of Benjamin's patients on that street was a retired merchant seaman named Larry Roberts, a double amputee who had spent the night of Hurricane Katrina floating on a couch near the ceiling of his home. He had phoned for help, which didn't come until morning, when a shrimp boat serving as a rescue vessel docked at his porch. With four feet of water already in his house, Roberts had managed to get himself to the living room and climb onto the couch as the water kept rising. The couch soon floated all the way to the ceiling, but fortunately for Roberts, the wind blew away a part of his roof, which enabled him to breathe. He spent the night that way, floating in the place where the roof had disappeared, as the wind and the rain were howling all around him.

"No, I wasn't scared," he insisted. "I'm a merchant marine. This wasn't the first time I'd been through a storm."

While Grace Scire could appreciate his nerve, she was afraid that the next time he wouldn't be so lucky. And she also knew there were Asian families for whom language barriers were always a problem. After Katrina, reporter Russ Henderson of the *Mobile Register* wrote about Hung Nguyen, a Vietnamese father who was warned by police the day before the storm that he should evacuate his home. Nguyen smiled politely, but he didn't understand. He relied on his daughter Loan Vo for English translation, and when the police came by, she was away from the house with her mother.

Scire, among others, thought it was crucial to develop a better plan, but as the second anniversary of Katrina was approaching, things were still in an unsettled state. To Tommy Reynoso, the building inspector for Bayou La Batre, the long-term solution was obvious—to build new housing outside the flood zone. "We are trying to get people out of low-lying areas," he said. "These storms in the last several years have taken a lot of the fight away. Katrina showed people how bad it can get, and really it could have been even worse. It *was* worse in parts of Mississippi and Louisiana. We don't want to go through this again."

By the summer of 2007, after several false starts, the city had bought more than sixty acres in the northern part of town several miles from the flood-prone areas. With a $17 million federal grant, officials were planning to build more than a hundred affordably priced homes. "These houses will have two, three, or four bedrooms and will cost ninety to a hundred thousand dollars, maybe a little more, depending on the size," Reynoso explained. "The neighborhood will have sidewalks, a small park, underground utilities, and it will be close to Alma Bryant High School. It's going to be nice."

He said the town also was talking with Boat People S.O.S. about a new neighborhood for Asian families, where homes would be even less expensive and refugees could still live close together as they had in the past. But Reynoso admitted that all of these things represented major change. Historically in the Bayou, people had lived within walking distance of the water, which had made it easy to get to their boats or to early-morning jobs at the seafood shops. But if the city's plans for rebuilding came together, life in the Bayou would not be the same.

"The mayor does not want to give up this heritage," said Reynoso. "We want to keep it a small fishing village, but it's going to have a different look. . . . There are hard and painful choices ahead. The painfulness is just getting started."

For some of the residents of Bayou La Batre, the rebuilding plans resurrected a deep unease, a fundamental division within the community about exactly what the future ought to look like. "The mayor," declared Larry Roberts, the retired merchant seaman, "has got this whole town turned upside down."

Speaking in an interview in 2007, Roberts gave voice to a local debate that had rumbled for the better part of two years. When developer Tim James unveiled his plans in 2005, several months before the hurricane, there were artists' renderings on display at city hall. The plans looked impressive—a high-end recasting of the local waterfront with boardwalks and spas, condos and coffee shops, and as one local newspaper article put it, "a flower-filled park under the shade of live oaks." At the heart of James's proposal, which carried a price tag of $200 million, was a high-rise condominium on land where the bayou emptied into open water.

In many ways, James's timing was superb. When he made his official presentation in the spring, everybody knew that Bayou La Batre was a community in trouble. Even before the devastation of Katrina, gas prices were rising, shrimp prices were dropping, and the heart of downtown was no longer the bustling place it had been. "A lot of people have problems with condos and such," Bayou shrimper Doug Johnson told the *Mobile Register*: "But I'd rather see (the town) go that way than go vacant." And Cyndi Johnson, a shrimper's wife, added another cautious note of interest: "There's a lot of hunger here for something new to happen. People know seafood can't hold us up by itself anymore."

By the middle of the summer, however, when James made the two-hour trip from his office in Greenville, Alabama, to continue his negotiations with the town, there was also the stubborn voice of opposition. At a public meeting on July 13, James had just agreed to pay $10.3 million for a crucial spit of land on Mississippi Sound when a member of the community on a fixed income got up to speak. "You can throw around a figure like $10 million," said Charlie Durden, "but what does it

The Wintzell Bridge rises above the waterfront in Bayou La Batre. Developers have proposed putting condominiums nearby.

© 1998 Sheila Hagler

mean to people like me? If the value of my home goes up, I won't be able to afford my taxes."

At first, James seemed genuinely astonished, having rarely, if ever, met anyone who didn't want their property values to rise. "It's the American way!" he declared.

And there it was—the clash of perspectives, of basic worldviews, that became much more apparent after Hurricane Katrina. Though James insisted that he wanted his plans to coexist with the traditional culture of the area, not to replace it, public skepticism erupted like a geyser on a cold winter night in 2006. On January 12, the city council met to consider a new zoning ordinance. The eighty-page proposal from the local planning board would have created a "marine resort" zone along the shore of the bayou—an area set aside for condos, houses, and upscale development. The shipyards, loading docks, and seafood houses that were already there—the traditional businesses of Bayou La Batre—would be declared "nonconforming" and not allowed to expand their operations. And if a nonconforming business stopped operating for six months—perhaps in the wake of a future hurricane—or if it sustained damages of more than 50 percent, its zoning would change and it would not be allowed to reopen.

Faced with a fury of public opposition, the council voted to table the proposal. "If we passed this, we might as well get a bulldozer and shove down all the business in Bayou La Batre," said Mayor Stan Wright. And one local business owner was even more pointed. "There would have been some killing," he said, "if this thing had passed."

And yet the larger issue remained unsettled. With a reeling economy and a devastated landscape, what was the realistic way to rebuild? To try to address that fundamental question, the mayor and city council brought in consultants from the Urban Land Institute (ULI), a nonprofit agency in Washington, D.C. The eleven-member panel came to the Bayou a year after Katrina, touring the waterways and the town. After a weeklong visit, the consultants came out strongly against the Tim James project, especially the idea of high-rise condos at the mouth of the bayou, blocking public access to Mississippi Sound. The panel members urged a more modest approach, one that would retain the traditional character of the village. They saw the possibility of ecocultural tourism: a refurbished waterfront, with pleasure boats moored beside the shrimping fleet, and tours of the nearby coastal savannah—and perhaps also of the seafood plants and local shipyards.

After receiving those recommendations, Mayor Wright announced that the Tim James plan was now on hold. "I don't want to seem ungrateful," he told the *Mobile Register*, "but Tim's not going to be in the driver's seat anymore."

Researcher Ty Keller, studying hurricane recovery for the Public Affairs Research Council of Louisiana, concluded that the ULI report "caused a sea change in the city's thinking. By October 2006, the mayor and city council had decided not to sell the city's waterfront property," Keller wrote. "Instead, they were considering leasing the land for a smaller development and limiting building heights to as few as three stories." Writing at the same time about the future of the Bayou, reporter Russ Henderson of the *Mobile Register* quoted planning experts who concluded, "Bayou La Batre can become one of those distinctive places that retain their identity while courting visitors, like Santa Fe, N.M." And he quoted Kathy Gazzier, who works in her family's Bayou shipyard, about her response to such a possibility: "That's music to our ears," she said.

But was it, in fact, a realistic vision, and was it really what the city leaders wanted? As the second anniversary of Katrina approached, and the vacant spaces grew larger downtown, the fear still rumbled beneath the surface that the traditional residents were being pushed aside. The unanswered question, two years after the catastrophic storm, was whether the town could find a delicate balance between injecting new life and tearing out the old.

To many of the residents of Bayou La Batre, the future somehow seemed almost as cloudy as the day Katrina came roaring through the town.

And then there was Coden. An unincorporated area just east of the Bayou, it stretched and sprawled along a coastline nearly startling in its beauty—sunlight glinting off of gray-blue water and patches of marsh grass set against the tide. A hundred years ago, this was the place of grand hotels, where the tourists came from far and wide and waded in the shallow, pristine surf. But the hotels were gone, and Coden had changed. Just before Katrina, there had been a row of handsome beach houses lining the shoreline, many of them shaded by live oak trees dating to the early history of the place. But with a few exceptions, the storm surge washed those houses away, reducing them to slabs or a stubble of posts, and while some of the families had decided to rebuild—elevating new houses on reinforced stilts—others concluded it was not worth the risk.

That was a part of the story of Coden—a story of elegance and fading grandeur, with a written history going back to the eighteenth century. But there is another reality in Coden as well, much of it hidden in the bayous and forests that stretch out eastward toward Mobile Bay. The official geography is imprecise, and only the locals can tell you where Coden starts and stops, and where Heron Bay, Sans Souci, and other unincorporated communities begin. And yet there's a palpable sense of common ground that links these struggling Alabama villages regardless of the race or circumstances of their inhabitants. And almost everybody will tell you that the feeling is stronger after Hurricane Katrina.

For many of the people, their poverty was already deeply entrenched before the physical battering of the storm, but two years later it has only gotten worse—reaching a level of desperation that is difficult for many outsiders to fathom. Indeed,

A pelican soars over the waters of Mississippi Sound, just to the south of Coden beach.

for the most part, the outsiders never see it; they never see the twelve-year-old girl with sandy blond hair and a beautiful smile who makes the trek periodically through three miles of woods to get from her father's trailer to her mother's house, which is built of wood and tarpaper siding, with windows still boarded up from the storm. Her teachers say she's a talented student, taking mostly accelerated classes, even though on most afternoons, as soon as the school bus stops near her house, she walks to the crab shop just up the road and works until dark. There's another family a few miles away, three generations crowded into a house where the window screens were blown away by Katrina and have not been replaced because the family can't afford it. There are medical problems that are far more pressing, ranging from epilepsy to asthma, but when you ask the grandmother how things are going, she will smile and say, "It's about the same, baby. We have to live with it." And then she will add for the sake of perspective that all of her fruit trees are doing very well.

She knows things are worse across the highway, where one family lives in a rusty school bus with a blue tarp covering the broken windows, and as a desperate concession to the thick coastal heat, an air conditioner replacing the glass in another. Barbara Reid, a Coden activist, says that whenever she goes to this part of the world, which many of the locals call Hard Luck City, she thinks about the quote from Joseph Bosarge, when he applied for his land grant in 1786: "to conceal from the eyes of everybody his poverty and misery." More than two centuries later, hidden deep in the woods, these are still proud people, Reid says, seafood workers, in many cases, who eke out a living on their oyster boats and certainly do not want anybody's pity. But Reid is angry at the official neglect, which she says has made their lives even harder.

It's a problem, she adds, afflicting most of Coden.

Reid is not alone in that view. In its dispassionate study of hurricane recovery, issued in April 2007, the Public Affairs Research Council took note of the "friction" between Bayou La Batre and the surrounding communities because of the "concentration" of federal assistance in the Bayou. "While the city (Bayou La Batre) has fewer than 2,000 residents at present," the council reported, "the greater Mobile Bay area has thousands more residents who, because they live in unincorporated areas, had no institutional mechanism for applying for grants. The Coden community, which has no formal boundaries, consists of 3,600 people in several hamlets lying south of Bayou La Batre: Alabama Port, Bayou Shores, Fowl River, Heron Bay, Portersville, Sans Souci and Coden. These unincorporated areas were ineligible for FEMA public assistance grants or CDBG (Community Development Block Grant) money, although residents did receive FEMA individual assistance money.

"The rural residents in the southernmost part of Mobile County also believe that the structure of the county governing body—a three-member commission elected from districts—had worked against their receiving adequate attention."

Beneath the measured words of that nonprofit study lies a seething controversy that erupted immediately after Katrina and has not abated in the two years since. Edwina Bates, a red-haired activist who grew up in Coden and Bayou La Batre and understood the cultural ties between the two, said Katrina and its aftermath stirred a renewed awareness of the division: a feeling of abandonment in Coden while help poured into Bayou La Batre. Today, Bates lives on the Coden side of the invisible line and is angry at the things she has seen all around her.

"Four elderly women in my neighborhood," she says, "all died in FEMA trailers or living with someone else. Every single one of those women gave up hope because they could never receive assistance to rebuild what they had. It was uncalled for. There is no justification for any of that."

But beyond the immediate aftermath, Bates is concerned about the shape of the future. Ranking near the top of her list of worries is the Bayou's plan to build a new sewage plant. She knows it is needed; the Bayou's old plant has long been strained beyond its capacity and is under court order to improve its facilities and eliminate spills. In the aftermath of Katrina, the U.S. Department of Housing and Urban Development awarded the town a grant of $24 million to build a new plant. Officials planned to put it in Coden, on an unincorporated patch of ground east of the Bayou and just north of open water. For people like Bates who live nearby, the plan raised strong environmental worries—the possibility, for example, that the plant could flood in a future hurricane, and that it would, inevitably, add to the pollution of Mississippi Sound, where this part of the Gulf washes against the shoreline of Coden. Already there were signs, not far from where the hotels used to be, offering a warning about polluted waters: TAKING OYSTERS BEYOND THIS POINT IS PROHIBITED — ALABAMA DEPARTMENT OF HEALTH.

"The old folks were more respectful of the environment," said Bates. "They knew where to put their septic tanks, how to keep the water clean; my grandmother didn't know how to read, but these were smart people. They said, 'Let's respect what has always been here.' They loved the serenity that goes with the history, the fact that it was a place where you knew your neighbors and where there were extended families all around. People were laid-back. They had little oyster boats and fishing boats; they were kind of like the Indians were—never taking more than what they needed.

"I think people today want to get back to who they were. They just don't know quite how to get there."

It is not that Bates and other grassroots activists are opposed to any form of development. It's clear the local economy needs a boost, and Bates, among others, is intrigued by the "ecofriendly tourism" that had been widely talked about in recent months. "But you can't trust the civic leadership in Bayou La Batre," she declared in an interview in 2007, "environmentally, number one, and historically, number two. Their concern is the dollar—bringing income to the city itself. And a lot of beautiful area is destroyed."

And so it was that as the second anniversary of Katrina was approaching, a sense of distrust and community division was one of the defining realities of the area—an impediment that remained to be overcome. But community leaders had reason to be optimistic. In addition to the monetary resources—at least $55 million in federal money and thousands more in private charity, which could still be distributed in an equitable way—there were also the lessons of history and character. Some of the old salts still remembered a time, from the 1930s to the 1950s, when artists' colonies flourished in the Bayou area, and this cultural tourism coexisted peacefully with the fishing fleet. The artists came in the spring, summer, and fall, producing a colorful body of work, with images taken from the Bayou landscape.

"Spring has come to Bayou La Batre," Genevieve Southerland, a painter from Mobile, wrote in 1947. "Wild violets are blooming around our cottage, the trees are budding, and all the landscape is beckoning to painters."

And one historian reported: "Painters set up their easels on the 'ox-bow' curves of the river bank to capture a view of the boats as they set out to sea."

Sixty years later, some community leaders in the Bayou area, inspired in part by the Urban Land Institute, thought they saw remnants of the same kind of charm—a promotable resource rooted in the very essence of the place. They knew the shrimp industry was still in decline; imported shrimp were pouring in from overseas, gas prices were worse than they had ever been, and after an encouraging catch just after Katrina, the shrimp nets once again were not as full. Crab and oyster production was solid, and shipbuilding continued at a steady pace. But tourists had been a part of the economy in the past, and there was the cautious hope that they could be again, "if we can get through the summer without a hurricane," said Mayor Stan Wright in 2007.

It was a hot day in July as the mayor settled back in his governmental office and talked about the ongoing problems of his town. His pickup truck, a 1998 Ford, was parked outside, and he was dressed, as usual, in faded work clothes more suited to his oyster shop than city hall. A large, good-humored man, suntanned from a life mostly spent outdoors, he found himself charged after Hurricane Katrina with the complicated task of leading the recovery. On this particular day in July, he spoke first about plans for affordable housing, with priority for people still in FEMA trailers—beginning with residents of Bayou La Batre, then the people in the area around it.

He also talked about the issue of development, a central ingredient in his vision for the future. "We had some high hopes," he said, speaking primarily of the Tim James project. "Seems like they all faded away." He said, however, there might be lessons from other communities, particularly Carrabelle, Florida, some three hundred miles down the coast, where residents have tried to mix new development with the remnants of their seafood industry.

"We got to preserve our industry that's here," said Wright. "But if a developer builds, there will be a domino effect"—especially with regard to restaurants, shops, and other retail that could help to revitalize downtown. That remained his article of faith, his belief in development as a path to better times, based on the premise that Bayou La Batre is "the last, best-kept secret on the Gulf Coast."

There were, of course, people who looked askance at that vision, who could see what developers had done through the years to other scenic parts of the Alabama coast. Across Mobile Bay, in the Baldwin County resorts of Gulf Shores and Orange Beach, high-rise condominiums now littered the landscape, obliterating the once rustic character of the beaches. And whatever the economic benefits, the cultural and aesthetic devastation was clear. For the ordinary residents of the Bayou and Coden, whose family roots ran deep into history, that was not a fate to be taken

Shipbuilding, long one of the staples of the Bayou economy, continues to flourish after Hurricane Katrina.

The *Bristol Leader*, an ocean-going craft, is nearing completion at a local shipyard.

lightly. But there was also the need for some kind of change, for an infusion of new economic life, and so in the conversations around town, there was still the hope for some kind of balance.

As the months went by, people quietly debated these issues and occasionally took their concerns to city hall. But mostly what they did was keep on pushing. Lisa Creal was one of those people. She was a high school senior in 2007, who graduated and immediately enrolled in Mississippi Gulf Coast Community College, hoping to pursue a career in nursing. After Katrina, which devastated her home, she and her family spent more than a year in a FEMA trailer. All of them tried to make the best of it—her father, her mother, her brother, and herself—though the ordeal was sometimes hard on her brother, a sixth-grader with asthma. Every night, they would fold the couch and table into beds, sometimes laughing at the absurdity of it all, and try to find as much comfort as they could.

"We'll always remember it," Lisa said of the trailer. "We were blessed to have it."

Tyler Kittles, who lived a few miles away, understood that spirit—that uncomplaining grit of people who understood what it meant to persevere. It's a quality that cuts across the generations, and Kittles saw it often when he was growing up, working the shrimp boats and then starting a cabinetmaking business of his own.

By the year 2000, Kittles had gained a reputation for his skill with his hands, when suddenly his life turned upside down. He was riding his motorcycle one day, bumping through the potholes of Shell Belt Road as it curved along the eastern side of the bayou. According to the police reports, he was traveling no more than 15 miles per hour, when he somehow managed to flip his bike and land on his head. Mayor Stan Wright was one of the first on the scene, and he found Kittles unconscious and unable to breathe, the strap from his helmet wrapped tightly around his neck. Wright reached immediately for his pocketknife and cut the helmet strap. Kittles later marveled at the gumption that it took, wondering if there was another

In the winter of 2006, Floyd Bosarge's last boat stands partially finished in his boat-building shed.

public official in the country who would have taken such a risk, given the litigious climate of the times. But that, Kittles thought, was Bayou La Batre, a place where people knew how to be neighbors and were willing to do what needed to be done.

And yet it was not until later—more than five months later—that Kittles had a chance to consider such things, for it took him that long to emerge from a coma. When he finally awoke, he was partially paralyzed and unable to speak, his brain stem damaged by the injury to his neck. "Physically, I was like an infant," he says, "but with the thoughts and memories of a thirty-year-old man." As soon as he could, Kittles entered into rehab and slowly, painfully, regained his speech and the large motor movements in most of his body. But his woodworking skills were a thing of the past, for the precision in his hands, particularly his right hand, could not be recovered.

In search of something to do with his life, he threw himself into the world of the mind, setting off in pursuit of a college degree, and studying the great American writers—from Herman Melville to William Faulkner and Harper Lee. He was often amazed by the power of their words, and after a time he was almost grateful for the twist of fate that had sent him their way. And yet he knew that the tenacity it took for his own recovery would not have been possible without his role models right there on the Bayou—those weather-beaten men who made their living from the sea and taught him what it meant to be strong.

He had seen them battle through storms, recessions, and their personal moments of hardship and tragedy. And they did it with patience and grace. There was a toughness rooted in a deep sense of place, and Kittles saw it in people like Floyd Bosarge, the grizzled boat-builder who had made a steady living with his hands. For more than half a century, Mr. Floyd had earned the admiration of his neighbors and provided an anchor for the bayou community, partly through his Monday night fish fries. At five o'clock without fail, his friends would gather from up and down the coast in the tin-roofed shed out behind his house, and Kittles, occasionally, was the youngest member of the group. He loved these older men and their stories—seafaring tales that grew into legends and then into myths, capturing the essence of life in their town. Mr. Floyd especially was one of his favorites. Like the others who came to the fish fry, the old storyteller embodied the steady work ethic of his place—a deep-seated feeling, as Kittles later put it, "that the fruits of your labor would roughly equal the amount of your effort."

Amazingly, that ethic had survived; had flourished, in fact, for two hundred years, and probably even longer, going back all the way to the days of the Indians. Kittles wasn't sure that anything could kill it, not the hardships of Hurricane Katrina, not a failing economy; not even the developers, if the community decided to go in that direction. At least not right away. But he worried that the ethic in a treasured way of life might slowly fade in the next generations, as the global markets and the battering of storms gradually, inexorably exacted their toll. That was a fear that many people shared.

Still there was hope. For the next five years the major hurricanes stayed away, but then in April, 2010, the BP oil spill created a whole new climate of doubt. An entire seafood season was lost, and though some families found work on the cleanup crews, and others received a modest compensation from BP, everywhere there were stories of hardship and loss. Eventually, however, the seafood beds re-opened and the shrimpers and oystermen returned to their boats; and perhaps against all logic and reason, the hope remained that the Bayou culture—that battered self-reliance with its ties to the sea—might be stubborn enough to survive.

Appendix—*Bayou Voices*

For anyone who seeks to understand the Bayou and the communities around it, there is no better way than listening to the voices of the people themselves. The following are a few of the most eloquent.

Julian Lee Rayford, author, *Whistlin' Woman and Crowin' Hen—*

You cannot comprehend the superlative quality of this town until you have seen the Bayou, the Bayou itself, that wrinkled, crumpled skin on the lacquered water. Early in the morning, there is a peace, a quiet in the marshes that cannot be disturbed even by the roaring of the engines of the boats. The trees are so dense that behind the wall of foliage it is like night. In that morning stillness, the sun breaks over a range of clouds that look like mountains. The whole area of the Sun is a pale yellow. Puffs of purple stand above the sun, and all the rest of the sky is blue-grey and promising to become white with the advancing day. . . .

Some mornings, the Bayou is so intensely green and clean, with a savage, fierce cleanness . . . like an animal or a bird that is always preening itself.

Granite Marker at St. Margaret's Catholic Church,
Prayer for the Blessing of the Fleet—

God bless your going out and your coming in; the Lord be with you at home and on the water. May he fill your nets abundantly as a reward for your labor; and may he bring you safely in, when you turn your boats homeward to shore.

Alma Bryant, revered Bayou educator, reflecting on the hurricane of 1906, which roared through the Bayou when she was thirteen; from the *Bayou Anthology*—

The most lasting impression on my life was made upon me when I watched Papa and Mama survey the devastation of their home. Looking tearfully into Papa's face, Mama asked, "Johnny, what are we going to do?" Seriously and serenely he scanned the disfigured area. Then he answered, "First we are going to thank God that our family is safe. Thirty-eight people, some of whom were our neighbors and friends, have lost their lives. This is our home. Here we came when we were married. Here our seven children were born. We'll build again." And build again they did, room by room until our eight-room house was restored. And because Papa and Mama possessed faith and courage, matched with unflagging industry, they built well.

Bayou old-timer Cecil Bosarge
poses for the camera with his latest catch.
© 2006 Sheila Hagler

Rodney Lyons, Bayou native, remembering how his neighbor
Alma Bryant and her brother George Bryant, an educator and artist,
made their gumbo—

Back in the late sixties, early seventies, Miss Alma and Mr. George Bryant lived together in the house. It was in their later years. Miss Alma would make gumbo once in a while. If she made oyster gumbo, she would send Mr. George down to our oyster shop with a five-gallon mop bucket, and when we'd drop a gallon of oysters on the screen to wash them off, he would put his bucket under the stainless steel screen to catch the water, and he would keep doing that until he would get a bucket full. He would take the bucket to Miss Alma and she would spend several hours straining this water 'til she got it real clean, and that's the water she used to make gumbo, because she would not use anything unless it had the natural taste. And when she made shrimp gumbo, she would make Mr. George save the heads and she's boil the heads in the water and then she's strain it down, and that's what she's use for a stock to make shrimp gumbo.

Miller Johnson, Heron Bay oysterman, from *The Bayou Anthology*—

I was born July 27, 1927. . . . I did a lot of bird hunting when I was a boy with a sling shot. I broke up old cast iron with a hammer. Mama made me a bag; I call it my slug bag. I tied it around my waist and put my slugs in it. I carried this old sling shot wherever I went. I shot a lot of robins and meadow larks with this hunting gear. Sometimes I would bring home 25 or 30 birds. I cleaned and washed them, Mama cooked them with rice. Back then you'd eat most anything. We ate a lot of old goats, turtles, mullet, oysters, crabs and most anything to fill your gut. In the summer time, on a clear day, we would walk down that old dry, hot, dusty road from the hill and get a skiff and go down to the bayou. Daddy would throw a cast net and catch mullet. We swam up oysters. We spent the whole day down on the bay, then we had to walk back up the road. We'd be so tired we could hardly take time to wash and go to bed. You see in the summer time, back then, there wasn't anything else to do. In the winter time things were different. Daddy would tong oysters and he had an oyster shop. Of course, he and Mama worked together. He tonged the oysters and Mama opened them and then Daddy hauled them to Mobile in the car, after he got one. . . .

I can feel fall in the air. Most of the men in Heron Bay would be tonging oysters by now, for that was what we made our living at. You could hear the roar of the boat motors echo through the old pine trees early in the morning before day break. For we wanted to be on the reef by sunrise. We worked all day and was back in the bayou at sundown. Most all the women opened oysters back then. If for some reason the man couldn't go out, then he helped open the oysters. It was a team thing and still is for some. A lot has changed since then. I live life one day at a time. . . .

But I'd rather tong oysters than be President of the United States.

Chanta Mak—Bayou La Batre student, from a sixth-grade paper at Alba Middle School—

My grandpa's name is Savunn. He lived in Cambodia. He was a soldier during the Khmer Rouge. He died in the year of the Cambodian War, but I don't know what his age was when he passed away. I didn't get to see him because I wasn't alive.

His hobby was to run down the street or dirt road to lose some weight and get strong. My grandma thinks about him every single night. She prays to him to have fun in the white clouds. My grandma dreams about him, saying, "Take care of our daughter and son-in-law." He wants us to have a good life.

His second hobby was to cut and carve wood. He made my grandma a stone to remind her that he would be with her always in this stone. But my grandma lost the stone during the time my grandpa was shot to death. I really want to know how he looked. He was a great man.

From *Alabama: A Guide to the Deep South*, produced just before World War II by the WPA (Works Progress Administration)—

BAYOU LA BATRE (pop. 964), a small community of winding streets and cottages set in gardens of roses, poppies, geraniums, larkspur and golden glow. Small musty shops, dim with age, are reminiscent of a Basque village. The road curves down to a water front littered with piles of oyster shells dumped by the canning factories where many of the townsfolk work. Smelly oyster and shrimp boats, their scarred hulls salt-stained and drab with age, crowd the shore line while discharging cargoes, or rock quietly at anchor in the bayou.

CODEN (pop. 300), a resort and fishing village on Bayou Coden. . . . The quaint white-painted Catholic church and the ramshackle oyster houses stand beside the bayou where boats discharge their daily catches. The scene is especially beautiful at sunset.

Peggy Denniston, Bayou La Batre teacher and writer, from
Eyes of the Storm: A Community Survives after Katrina—

On August 28, 2005, the people of Bayou La Batre heaved a huge sigh of relief. It looked like Hurricane Katrina was headed to Grand Isle, Louisiana, almost 200 miles west. Everyone had prepared for this storm, just like the summer when Ivan the Terrible paused off shore and battered them before heading east, a blessed little turn of fate. Nobody had any idea that Katrina would wipe out nearly 300 miles of the Gulf Coast. On August 29, the eye of the deadliest storm of a century rammed Grand Isle, leaving nothing standing, and took a slight turn east, headed straight for Mississippi. Ground Zero got closer to the Bayou.

Hurricanes are just part of living on the Gulf Coast, as is watching projected tracks. East of the eye is the bad side of a storm, where the winds and water slam into land. The Bayou had weathered a list of recent storms, three already in the summer of 2005, and a dozen in the last decade. Trees had already fallen, families had preparations down to a routine, and mooring boats to century-old oak trees had been practiced all summer long. People batten down belongings and prepare to survive for weeks after a storm, without electricity or open stores, without clean water or ice to refresh long hot days of dealing with repairs and debris. But nobody was prepared for Katrina.

Water, more so than wind, took Bayou La Batre by surprise. Not a building in a fishing village that makes its living from the sea escaped damage, how ironic. Nearly twenty feet of water swept through Coden, the community south of town, and crested miles north of the coast, creating a boat launch for rescuers in Food Tiger's parking lot. Many who evacuated returned to houses still standing, but barely. As Aline Seaman, 84, said, "The water just kept coming. That's when I left, but I returned to a house full of mud and diesel fuel, with everything topsy-turvy." Her house, where she's lived since 1939 and raised nine children, floated off its cinder blocks and everything inside rose only to collapse in heaps of filth. Like so many others, it's beyond repair, but she sits in a rocker in her former living room each day, not able to let go of her home.

After the flooding began, Katrina's wind roared into Alabama about midnight, transformers exploded with sparks flying in sideways rain, and electrical power was cut to most of Mobile County. Huge pines slammed to the ground, without warning, from a vertical stance to horizontal in milliseconds. Roofs blew away, ships that weren't lashed to multiple oaks sloshed onto land, and tornados spun off and wiped out neighborhoods—especially trailer parks. Even so, the wind didn't compare to the relentless storm surge. The Gulf of Mexico became an enormous swirl of water with no place to go but ashore. The people of the Gulf Coast compare Katrina to Camille—the one that destroyed Mississippi in the 1960s—but Katrina was worse, more like the unnamed storm that destroyed this area in 1906. Katrina was the storm of the century.

Jada Davis, Bayou La Batre student, "Katrina's Pain," from
Eyes of the Storm: A Community Survives after Katrina—

> My house crowded with relatives
> Who lost their homes in the Bayou.
> We sat in the heat
> With no power or water for weeks.

My house wasn't damaged much,

But homes all around us were destroyed.

Pets were lost.

Trees blocked the road.

The aftermath was devastating.

Stores were closed for a long time.

Gas went way up

And tempers flared in the heat.

Elsie Simmons, former library clerk from Coden, from an interview with the authors—

Katrina destroyed everything we had but the house. I live on Hemley Road in Coden. We were totally flooded with four and a half feet of water. It was the first time in the fifty years we had lived in that house that the water ever came that far. They say it came to where we live in '06, but not since then. With Katrina, you'd see people's belongings in the tops of trees, and it would break your heart. In the black community of Coden, a lot of people have left because of how it destroyed their homes so bad. On Midway Street, there are seven families that are just gone. They couldn't get the help to rebuild.

I think Katrina has destroyed our community and it's a big loss. The old people started dying out, and the young people started leaving, and this was a good place too. We had big families back when I was coming up, and I don't know a day we went hungry. We never had welfare, never got food stamps, never ate a free lunch in school. And we all went to school, and our parents worked hard and expected us to do the same. I admired the way we were brought up. You would never find cleaner homes, and we weren't any haters. Coming up, we all played together; it didn't matter who you were, and we were raised by the whole community, not just our parents.

People here had a lot of wisdom. This was a strong, close-knit community.

Phillip Morris, lifelong Coden resident, talking about the destruction of his house during Hurricane Katrina; from an interview with his daughter-in-law, Sandra Morris—

I had a little dog in there, and the lights went out before daylight. I shined a flashlight on that water in the back; it was way up to the back steps, and it was clear as a crystal. Usually when the storm comes in, it's muddy. That ought to have been my clue. I said, "I can't believe it." That little dog, I had it in the dining room. Them other two dogs, after a while, got up under the house. I shined that light, looking; they'd go back under there and come back out. What they was telling me, "There's water under the house."

I opened the door. I said, "Come on in then." I say, "Y'all lay down. . . ." I went through the dining room. I was going to shine on the front porch, see if the porch was still on it. It was blowing pretty good by then. When I went back through there, there was a big ole bulge in the dining room, under the rug. That little dog done moved from where she was at; she was down by the ice box. I said, "Boy, that thing is coming in fast." The water was up under that rug. I said, "Well, I'm gon' take that little dog upstairs." Them other dogs was in the dining room with me.

I took the dog upstairs, then I come downstairs, and the whole door blowed out. I tried to put the door back, couldn't do it, and then the windows busted out. The seas was coming in through the windows and the doors—wham, wham, one after the other. And the little dog come down the stairs and run out the door. I said, "That's a dead dog. I ain't going to be able to get her." So I had a plan. I run to the back door. I said, "That water's coming in here; I'll just let the water run out the back," and it did. But that little dog swam out the front, came back around and come back in the door that was open back there. She made it.

So anyway, everything was floating by then—kitchen, the dining room was floating. I could feel it floating. I had them other two dogs back in the kitchen and dining room. I went back upstairs. I said, "Man, I'm in trouble." I could feel the walls going, making all kinds of racket. . . . So I went upstairs, top of the stairs; there was a window there. After while, the kitchen broke away. It floated out there, and I seen a little dog in there. It broke the wall, and it unfolded like a book, and the top went down. That dog swum out before it fell on him. And that bulldog was swimming, and there was a strange dog come from over yonder. . . .

So I kept sitting there; the whole house was crying. The front door went, and all this marsh grass and junk was coming in the living room. And so, that strange dog swam up and I was standing there watching that little dog swimming. . . . He was looking for me all that time.

So the old house went to hollering and screaming, the front walls just a'flopping. I was sitting up at the top of the stairs; the water was coming in all the way to the top where I was at. After a while, the whole house just fell, just wham! And everything started falling on me. I said, "Now's the time for me to escape." So I just eased out the window. The tide by then was up to the top of the window. . . . I was going for that little tree yonder, but when I got overboard, the whole wall floated right in front of me. I said, "That's good enough." That little dog crawled up on it too. . . .

The water was a'boiling and a'whistling and the tide was going. . . . I went over the top of a school bus over there, and then I went by that big oak tree. I almost got in it, but the tide wasn't up enough for me to get in it. So when I crossed that bayou down there, something must have broke and it brought me back in towards these woods. . . . I finally got there and hung on top of an oak tree. Hours went by. It finally come up back out of the south, and boy it was a'whistling. You could hear it like motors running and everything. You could see it like a fog down there. So I said, "Little dog, I ain't gon' stay with you no longer. . . ."

Drift was coming down, I was pushing drift away from me all the time. I said, "That thing is going to push me out in the gulf. I got to get off the drift. I got to get off my wall." I went off through the woods. There wasn't no bottom . . . so I went about a hundred yards and I seen some stuff I recognized. . . . I said, "I might be could touch bottom here." I tried; I couldn't. I was about neck-deep then. I said, "If I can get back to that road," and there was so much drift, all jammed, that I had to come back in the woods and go around it. . . .

I finally got on the road and was walking on it and directly a big alligator broke there in front of me. . . . I scared that alligator, and then I couldn't see him. I knew he was laying there. Bubbles started coming up where he went down. So I give him plenty of room. I went on around him. I got up about twenty-five foot ahead of him and stepped on a flounder; fish and all was up that road. That scared me. I got out my pocket knife by the alligator, you know. I was planning on, if the alligator got me, I knew I was going to survive. I'd kill that alligator with the knife.

So I went on along, and then I could see shrimp jumping in front of me, all up that road, big ole white shrimp, all the way to Highway 188. I finally made it to the hill and then I had my truck all up on the hill where it wouldn't get wet. But it had gotten up to the windshield on it. . . . It got all my tools, lawnmower, weed-eaters. . . . I got in that truck and went to sleep, I was so tired, although it filled up with old mud and stuff. . . .

I lost my instruments and everything—banjos, Ralph Stanley records, and $4,200 worth of money I couldn't get. It's gone. Somebody find it or maybe they won't. But it could have been worser. A lot of folks got it worser.

Saphea Khan, Bayou La Batre student, "Five Thousand Dollars," from *Eyes of the Storm: A Community Survives after Katrina*—

Our family left on the night of the hurricane.
We almost didn't make it to the shelter.
We stood, looking out the window,
Watching shingles fly.

When we came home
We found our house full of filth,
And all our possessions scattered—
Covered with mud.

My dad used to take time
To make the best of his chickens,
But he lost every one of them.

My family spent a month

Eating canned food and MREs.

We still have no power in our original house,

And the FEMA trailer has a lot of outlet problems.

We lost everything

And FEMA offered us $5,000

Some people

Who did not even get damage to their homes

Got close to three times that much.

Tiffany Le, student at Alba Middle School, from a documentary coproduced by the University of South Alabama and students at Alma Bryant High School—

I am really happy where I am today. I have great teachers, great parents. . . . After Katrina, students just wanted to get back to school, all away from hurricane damage, and be with their teachers. Their teachers made us laugh, and we feel a lot better.

Jimmy Wigfield, Bayou La Batre native and assistant sports editor, the *Mobile Register*, from the February 17, 2007, *Mobile Register*, copyright 2007, reprinted with permission—

The front door around which Red Wigfield stuffed cotton wadding to keep out hurricane floodwaters is gone, obliterated by the soup of demons—a dark, rampaging wall of water that writhed with dead animals, furniture, tires, car parts, shingles, two-by-fours, trawl boards, concrete blocks and trees—conjured by Katrina, a storm he never saw.

The only evidence of the sign that once hung over that door and proudly proclaimed the establishment as Red's Service Drug is a corroded and battered metal brace.

Affixed to one of the surviving windows is a pink card that warns: "UNSAFE. Entry may result in death or injury," which is an astonishing departure from a place that for 25 years offered warmth, comfort and healing, as well as the finest milkshakes and hot doughnuts to be found.

The story is the same for the gutted building that occupies the first few hundred feet of Shell Belt Road and once housed a TV repair shop, grocery store, dry goods store and several restaurants. It has no place in the post-Katrina Bayou, so it will soon be pummeled into rubble, then cleared away, leaving nothing but memories.

Mr. Red—as my daddy was widely known—died 20 years ago from lung cancer, leaving an unpatchable hole in the lives of his family and his fellow townspeople because he was so compassionate, so cheerful, so full of integrity, so full of life. Take away a stint on a destroyer in the U.S. Navy during World War II and his college years at Auburn University learning how to be a pharmacist on the G.I. Bill, and he was rarely ever out of the Bayou. And the Bayou was never out of him, which is to say he developed an appreciation for hard work, a devotion to helping his fellow man, and learned how to get back up after being knocked down.

The first time I ever saw him cry—one of the few times I ever saw him cry—was when his drugstore got flooded out by Hurricane Camille in 1969. He lost nearly everything, but had enough left that he took badly needed drugs, bandages and supplies to Biloxi, where as a 7-year-old I saw bodies being pulled out of the treetops. He rebuilt, only to get flooded out again in 1979 by Frederick. Again, he came back.

The store hours were whenever to whenever. In the days before drive-through drugs and 24-hour chain pharmacies, my dad got calls in the middle of the night from a parent needing medicine for a sick baby or someone needing an emergency prescription filled. He would get up and go open the store because of a promise he had made.

"When we opened the store, he said he had a mission, and that was that no child would ever go without a prescription in this town that he knew of, even if the parents didn't have the ability or the desire to pay. He asked me if I'd agree to that and I said yes," recalled my mother, Betty, who kept the books for the store and still lives in Bayou La Batre.

When people couldn't pay, they would often offer him sacks of oysters, or boxes of shrimp, mullet and produce, and he would gladly accept them.

Despite the posted warning, I recently stepped through the doorway of the old drugstore, seeking to revisit those times when he presided from behind his prescription counter. Back then, he had attached a cowbell to the top of the door, and it pealed every time a customer arrived or departed.

This time, I heard only the crunch of shattered glass; this time, I saw a floor caked with dry swamp mud instead of shiny tile; this time, I smelled the muck and mildew instead of Granny Vel Carroll brewing coffee or making those cherry Cokes or banana splits at the soda fountain, or the faint aroma of perfumes that Helen Bosarge and Eva Mae Sprinkle offered as samples over the cosmetics counter.

One of the big front windows that exploded during Katrina once held a special painted message: "It's a boy . . . Lil Red," which proclaimed my arrival in December 1961 after being adopted. When my parents returned from Montgomery with me, they discovered that all the cigars in the drugstore were gone.

Forty-five years later, everything is gone.

Walking under drooping ceiling tiles, I approached what was always my favorite part of the store, the soda fountain. Only the walls remain, but in my mind's eye I can still see the chrome milkshake cups and the mixer, and the many little placards with witticisms that surrounded the counter, much like the ones in Wintzell's restaurants in Mobile. And above that were all of my dad's mounted trophy fish, especially some of the big speckled trout he caught. We liked to go fishing on the bayou in the mornings before I had to go to school and he had to open the store.

When he'd open the store, he'd often find a crowd, with shipyard and seafood workers stopping by to get coffee or hot doughnuts, which he and the store ladies made from scratch. I got to make my own milkshakes, although Granny Vel, who ruled the soda fountain, would often grump that I was using too much malt or chocolate syrup.

On some Sunday nights, my dad would proclaim that the supper menu would consist solely of Brown's Velvet ice cream, and he and I and my sister, Beth, would go open up the store and start packing cups full of it. Every now and then someone would come by and see the light on—"You open, Mr. Red?"—and want a milkshake or need something, maybe batteries, maybe pantyhose. The shakes were legendary; in fact, my dad would give them away to the Alba High School football players if they won.

A few steps to the right of the soda fountain was the entrance to a hallway, over which he would post the scores of the Auburn, Alabama and Alba football games on a marquee each season. He'd listen to the games on Saturdays on his trusty Zenith radio, which was perched on the shelf of his prescription counter. When I got big enough to finally climb the ladder and change the scores each week, I deemed it a huge responsibility. And while he loved Auburn, he and his Alabama friends traded friendly banter, nothing like the bitter and ugly exchanges often seen today.

His phone rang constantly, but he never seemed harried. It was normal to hear him whistling and talking while clacking away at the typewriter, preparing a label for another prescription. Nowadays, some pharmacists will tell you about the medication when you pick it up, and others will just let the corporate literature serve its clinical purpose. My dad would always engage customers in conversation before, during and after he filled prescriptions, setting their minds at ease. Often, he just asked about that person's life, or related a funny story. People usually left his store feeling better without swallowing a single pill.

I almost always felt good there, and in all of that little center of Bayou La Batre. Right across the street was the weekly *Mobile County News*, where the Rankin family and Herbert Johnson gave me my first journalism job when I was in the eighth grade. Jiffy Burger was right there. Homecoming and Christmas parades went by. My Aunt Gladys had a clothing store a few doors down.

There were a few times I didn't feel so good there, like when I kicked a catfish and the barb broke off in my foot, or when I got one of the worst whippings in my life when I was maybe 5 or 6. Miss Alma Bryant—who remains probably the most revered person in the south end of the county, a noted educator for whom Bryant High School is named and one of the friendliest people you would ever meet—came into the store and spoke to me. I told her to "Shut up, stupid."

I could have explained that I was only repeating words I had heard elsewhere, but I don't think it would have made any difference. Out of the corner of my eye I saw my dad—who had been one of Miss Alma's students during his school years—jump from behind his prescription counter and head straight for me. He then pulled my pants down and whipped me in the store, in front of everybody. Lesson in respect learned.

Some might think a little town like Bayou La Batre never had crime, that it was like Mayberry. But my daddy carried a revolver, which he had a permit for, at all times just in case of a robbery. Thankfully, he never had to use it, but the store was broken into a number of times in the middle of the night, with the thieves usually going for the narcotics. I would have gone for the milkshakes.

In later years whenever I went to see him at the store, we would usually visit at the side of the prescription counter, which was raised a foot or so off the floor. That way, he could still be taller than the little boy who had grown up under his guidance. He loved talking about sports, and was always curious about the places I had gone and the things I had seen, the coaches and players I met, the things that didn't make it into the newspaper. It was there on a December day in 1986 that he stood there, suddenly pale and older, and struggled to tell me he thought he had cancer. Three months later, he was gone, and a large part of the heart of old-fashioned Bayou La Batre went with him.

As I walked through the ruins of what was once his drugstore, I could hear his voice and smiled at the memories he left. Through the front windows, I saw a UPS truck, its brakes squealing, come to a sudden stop, dust from the street swirling about. I saw the driver looking hard at the building and shaking his head. For a moment, I let myself pretend he was making another delivery to Red's Service Drug. But he pulled away, moving on down the road, in the Bayou left by Katrina.

Tyler Kittles, Bayou La Batre resident and student, adapted from "Loomings," an English paper on Bayou La Batre, written at the University of South Alabama. (The title of the paper is borrowed from Chapter 1 of Herman Melville's *Moby Dick*)—

This place isn't mystical—it's home; every day I see reflections of who I am and what I stand for in the sea-salted and sun-baked weather-beaten faces, and hands calloused by generations of exposure to life's storms incurred in this tightly knit fishing village. Until an "outsider" remarks of the unique quality of something they have observed in Bayou La Batre (whether that thing be an attitude expressed, or a physical feature of the way of life), it virtually has never occurred to me that this is, in fact, unique; how could it? This place is home; I take it for granted—from the slow-tempo ratcheting of the large marine-diesel engines, to breakfasts of silver school mullet where the grease would be popping in the fryer (literally) even before the fish take that last choking gasp from the skiff's floor—not from a sense of "entitlement," but from a general sense of ignorance that the whole of society doesn't operate under the same construct; why should it occur to me that, in many ways, the general outlook on how to go about accomplishing the tasks of life is actually different down here? Sure, I read the newspaper and watch reports on TV about the pitiful condition of relations between (this or that) minority and the indigenous population, but this isn't my reality; mine has always been marked by a strong sense of community (consisting of all these communities), a commonality and deep-seated sense of shared purpose among races/ethnicities represented in a village of just over 2,000 inhabitants.

Bayou La Batre is a cultural gumbo where every ingredient is a stand-alone entity that lends its own unique texture to this ever-evolving recipe that (collectively) stakes its livelihood and reputation on shrimp, crabs, oysters, mullet; and the roux that binds all this diversity into a consolidated dish is acceptance. My intention is not to present this "dish" as some over-romanticized dramatic rendition of some human ideal; many of these ingredients are contradictory of one another and are insulting to the palate if allowed to dominate the stew. In order to guard against insult, an equitable balance (in this village) has always been sought. To make this "gumbo" even spicier, mix into this conglomerate a tremendous display of religious control from the Catholic Church, most of the major and many of the minor denominations of the Protestant Christian Church, and three Buddhist Temples, all vying for the "souls" of 2,000 people. It is a commonly known fact of humanity that if one wants to guarantee strife and unrest, combine contrasts along racial/ethnic and religious lines and place them all in the same pot in pursuit of the same ends: "survival." Why has it been, for the most part, a success here, where this same compound of volatile elements has resulted in explosion elsewhere? To do justice to a question as far-reaching and all-inclusive as the previous, one would need to enlist the leading talents in the professions of sociology, economics, psychology, and philosophy, and perhaps still not be able to arrive at a conclusion that would be of much use.

A parallel can obviously be made between the seafaring lifestyles of Bayou La Batre and that of the nineteenth-century New Bedford, Massachusetts, whaling fleet as portrayed in Herman Melville's classic novel *Moby Dick*; but then as one sounds the depths for further correlation, they become uncannily analogous: (1) both portray life reliant on the sea for survival; (2) both portray a people reliant on "wits" that have been honed to razor sharpness by daily exposure to life-threatening conditions at sea; (3) both portray a people reliant on the acceptance of diversity and the need to homogenize this diversity into a community where individual talents are to be utilized precisely where they will be most beneficial to survival of the community that resides (in microcosm) aboard the vessel.

Much like the fictional literary world aboard the *Pequod*, as captured by Melville, Bayou La Batre is far from a utopian society; like the community, as partly portrayed through the contrasting characters of the Christian Ishmael and the pagan Queequeg on the pages of *Moby Dick*, neither side is volunteering to share the same bed; but instead of allowing differences to escalate into mutiny and destruction of their society, they almost always deal with conflicts on the interior before these differences reach a level that requires outside interference. So, far from all players in this drama being gathered around the camp-fire singing "Kumbaya," there is, instead, an almost maniacal drive for success in the face of insurmountable odds: weather, global competition, deteriorating ecosystem, and increasing governmental regulation of an industry in its death throes; success, not necessarily by the world's standards, but by the only standards that really matter—their own. Success is a relative term; if one takes inventory of the multitude of challenges that collectively are exclusive to this community, it strikes most as indeed amazing that any people facing such difficulties would even attempt to weather the storm, much less be positively productive in most cases, and even victorious on occasion; whereas, a people not accustomed to "battening the hatches" and riding with a looming storm will lack the experience absolutely essential to survival under extreme conditions. You won't hear much protestation about the deplorable condition of such and such, because these people have been so habituated, for generations, to founding success precisely on conditions that, to an outsider, would seem a lost cause, but to the natives it's "just another day at the office."

An occupation by definition: a means by which one finances life, though here in Bayou La Batre and surrounding coastal villages these seafaring occupations seem to transcend to a different level (for better or worse); life is so intertwined with the occupation that they together represent a unit, where it is impossible to view even minute details of one without seeing reflections of the other deeply ingrained.

Down here occupations transcend to absolute obsession in order to prevail over these stacked odds that only seem to increase in intensity. In most cases, there is no one to call for assistance, for if this gale is too intense for your vessel, then the best way to ensure complete destruction is to involve another vessel, so each can pound the other to pieces; living daily under such conditions seems to deeply instill a profound level of self-reliance into the community as a whole.

The total reliance on the talents and abilities of the crew on board one's vessel (that are responsible for it making an all-around successful voyage) develops in most a deep-seated sense of identity, purpose, and self-worth; and who gives a rat's rear end about superficial differences in individual crew-members when life and limb are at stake? In vocations where the only stable horizon to be seen will be on a dashboard compass makes it is an absolute necessity that literal and figurative equilibrium be found and maintained on board; this fact inevitably shapes one's general outlook in other arenas as well: that the most sure means to weather a storm is to move with its energy, and be as prepared as possible to take positive advantage of any lulls when they occur. I feel that it was upon Melville's observation of this trait of moving with a storm's action, of this "live and let live" acceptance among other traits that parallel with those of present-day Bayou La Batre, that inspired the writing of one of the most studied pieces of classic American literature. If traits analogous even in part prompted Melville's writing of this novel, I think it would be safe to suppose that there may be, in reality, something here that also deserves study.

One of the essential ingredients almost at the heart of this "Bayou gumbo" that has ensured success for generations of locals is this: the young men (out of straight-up necessity) taking the helm, for the sake of the family, at an age absolutely unheard of in most other circumstances; in many societies children are allowed to be children almost indefinitely, not here; while it is never presented to the youngster in a fashion that invokes a sort of "god-complex" that often is developed when a young man is instantly served a level of authority before the respect (that must precede said authority) is ever actually earned. Respect and authority are of two completely different species; respect can never be gifted; and I feel that fact is deeply instilled into subsequent generations of any community subjected to such circumstances as can be witnessed in Bayou La Batre.

Although nothing brought up in this reflection qualifies as an earth-shaking revelation, it's nothing that I have ever devoted much time to contemplate in the past; this is home; why would it occur to me that the way of life in Bayou La Batre is, in any way, unique? This is all I've ever been exposed to on an intimate level; it's not until an observant outsider brings to my attention a facet of the lifestyle that lends identity to this place that I can appreciate it as some unique trait, and see it somewhat from their perspective that this is not, in fact, the "norm" everywhere you go. What keeps coming to mind that may offer a glimpse of the overall attitude held on life down here is a saying that has almost reached cliché status in and around this village that has eked out its existence for centuries from the sea; the subsequent aroma of this place, at times, is far from genteel; the locals' almost scripted response to an outsider's sickened revulsion to the perfume of decomposing sea-life is: "smells like money to me"; this serves as a generic representation of the outlook prevalent here in the Bayou: completely unpretentious about what may have to be done to pay the bills, and that holds true for every ingredient (regardless of its ethnicity) in this "Bayou Gumbo," from the captain/commander of the vessel to the lowest-ranking deckhand, it all smells like money for the whole crew/family/community; what is almost absent from the vocabulary of the people in this community is the term "demeaning"; there, by God, isn't time for pretension here.

A Bayou shrimp boat is all
decked out for the Blessing of the Fleet.
© 2007 Sheila Hagler

Koan Ang, teacher's aide, Mobile County Public Schools, from an interview with the authors—

I left Cambodia after the war, right after Communists took the country. We had government jobs. We knew we would be killed. On April 17, 1975, we fled to Thailand—my husband, my son, my daughter, and me. It was very frightening. My daughter, my baby, was about fifteen days old.

When we came here, we knew it was very safe for our kids. Both of them graduated from the University of South Alabama. My daughter is a doctor and my son is a mechanical engineer. My daughter was valedictorian in her high school. In college, she made straight A's in pre-med. We knew education was important. I feel all the kids need to understand about education. I try to work with them day by day.

After Katrina, I work with Lutheran Disaster, trying to build houses back. Some clients build back themselves; others have to apply for help. In Cambodia, we don't have deeds like U.S. has. Some families don't know about this. Some lost deeds in wind and water. We have to take them to the courthouse to record deeds and make sure everything is correct.

Some still live in FEMA trailers, even after all this time. But I feel we will still keep going and build back this place. In Cambodia, I lost forty-two people in my family during the war. It was a true killing field—forty-two killed in one night. My sister, brother, nephew, all killed in one night. I was in the hospital. I could not control myself. I had lost too much for one time, and it broke my nerves. But I am fine right now.

What problems we have now, we have to compare them to that.

Joey Nguyen, Bayou La Batre student, from a paper called "The Sunset," written at Alma Bryant High School—

I dread each and every day of my life, well a large majority of them at least. They all seem the same. I wake up and get ready for school, go to school, and then return home just to go to work. My life is indeed boring and not a bit exciting. Every day involves work or disappointment. It seems as if there's nothing that sparks my imagination or desire. . . .

Each day passes by so fast that I can't grasp what's around me. I'm about to graduate and it seems as if everything is coming to an end. I guess it just snuck up on me without my noticing, and in a flick of an eye it's all over.

Here I lie under the tree watching as the sun goes down. It's so peaceful and beautiful. I guess I never took the time to realize the world around me. Maybe everything is not as bad as I thought. Each day I can wake up with hope and happiness that this day brings another great sunset.

Sue Chanthapaseuth, resident of Bayou La Batre and caseworker for Boat People S.O.S., a committed advocate for the Asian community in the Bayou—

I am twenty-nine years old. This is my hometown. This is my work. I want to teach young people old customs so that they don't forget their heritage.

Notes and Acknowledgments

This book was made possible by the cooperation of the people of Bayou La Batre, Coden, and the other seafaring communities along the Alabama coast, where the residents have freely shared their stories. In the next several pages, we will acknowledge their contributions in detail, as well as those of other writers and scholars who have occasionally turned their attention to the Bayou. *Mobile Register* reporter Russ Henderson has done an especially fine job in the past several years, and we have relied on his dispatches, as well as those of other reporters at the paper.

We also relied on a very good summary of the Bayou's history written by long-time resident Juanita McRoy and published in *The Bayou Anthology*, compiled and edited by Troy Vesper with Arthur McRoy and Colleen Harrison, and published by the Bayou La Batre–Coden Historical Foundation. We commend the leaders and members of that organization for their efforts to keep local history alive. And finally, we read with delight the colorful book from the 1950s, *Whistlin' Woman and Crowin' Hen*, written by Mobile author Julian Lee Rayford.

But there was no substitute for personal interviews, and here, chapter by chapter, are all of the sources, both written and oral, that we have relied upon for the story.

Introduction—Life on the Edge

The overview of the hurricane of 1906 was pieced together, in part, from stories that appeared in the *Mobile Register*. On October 6, 2006, one of the paper's reporters, Cammie East Cowan, put together a special report on the storm of 1906, compiling quotes and descriptions from the coverage that appeared a century ago. The vivid recollections from Bayou educator Alma Bryant have appeared in several places, including *The Bayou Anthology*. The arresting description of Bayou survivors—"Most . . . resembled great chunks of liver-colored beef," was written by the late Mobile author George B. Toulmin and appeared in the *Mobile Register*, both at the time of the storm and in the more recent article by Cammie East Cowan.

The quotes from oysterman Avery Bates—"We love it like a farmer loves digging in the dirt"—came from an interview on October 17, 2006. Bates and many others in the Bayou, including Mayor Stan Wright, seafood processor Walton Kraver, and seafood broker Rodney Lyons, all offered their thoughts on the changing economic realities of the seafood industry, as did Robert Shipp, a marine biologist at the University of South Alabama. The fearful quote about development—"They are chomping at the bit to change this place"—came from Bayou resident Randy Schjott in an interview on October 16, 2006.

The description of Hurricane Katrina was based on accounts in the *Mobile Register*, as well as the personal experiences of the authors. The harrowing survival story of the Ngam family appeared in the *Mobile Register* on September 5, 2005, and was confirmed in later interviews with the authors. Rodney Lyons's ironic quote, "Katrina may have saved us," came in an interview on October 6, 2006.

1 — The Storytellers

Marie Gray's memories of the storm of 1916 appeared in written form in *The Bayou Anthology*, and Mrs. Gray recounted the moment in greater detail in an interview with the authors. Diane Silvia's account of Native American life in the Bayou appeared in an article titled "The Distinctive Character of a Bayou Community: Continuity and Change in Bayou La Batre from Prehistoric to Recent Times," *Gulf Coast Historical Review*, vol. 4, no. 1, published in the fall of 1988.

The story of Jean-Baptiste Baudreau has been pieced together from several sources, including vol. 1, chapter 12, of Albert James Pickett's *History of Alabama*, published in 1851; *Jean Baptiste and Henriette (A Creole Tragedy)*, copyright 1995 by Randall Ladiner; and from the Web site of the Portersville Revival Group, which featured the research of Portersville board member Barbara Jean McNamara. The official account of Baudreau's execution was quoted by Ladiner. (Because spellings in the eighteenth century had not been standardized, some sources refer to Baudreau as Baudrau or Baudrot.)

Joseph Bosarge's petition for a Spanish land grant in 1786 appears in full in Mary Louise Adkinson's *Bouzage Bosarge Family*, published in 1986 by the Mississippi Coast Historical and Genealogical Society. Adkinson's work also offers a readable summary of Bosarge's life. Julian Rayford's *Whistlin' Woman and Crowin' Hen* provides an excellent sense of the storytelling tradition in the Bayou and is the source for the story of the pirate Spud Thompson.

The records of Leslie Garner McRoy, who helped bury the dead after the hurricane of 1906, were preserved by his grandson Arthur McRoy and were quoted in the *Mobile Register* on November 10, 2005. Arthur McRoy's memories of the sound of shrimp boats "on a misty November morning" were shared in an interview on

September 29, 2006. Marie Schjott, one of the Bayou old-timers, shared stories of her life on October 16, 2006, as did her son Randy Schjott.

The story of the Rosenwald school for African American children in the community of Grand Bay, just west of the Bayou, was recounted in the *Mobile Register* on March 30, 2007. Three African American residents and leaders in the Bayou La Batre–Coden area—Nancy McCall, Elsie Simmons, and Ernestine Williams—shared the moving story of their ancestors in a series of interviews during the spring of 2007. Sakhoeum Kahn, a Cambodian teenager, offered her assessment of Bayou La Batre as "a welcoming town" during an interview with the authors on May 10, 2007.

Reporter Brendan Kirby of the *Mobile Register* covered the March 29, 2007, drug bust in Bayou La Batre, and his article appeared the following morning. The "send a message" quote from Bayou La Batre mayor Stan Wright appeared in that article. The authors interviewed Bayou octogenarian Lazarus Johnson, who expressed his disdain for local drug dealers, and we also attended several of Floyd Bosarge's fish fries, recording the stories that were told on those occasions. Sadly, we also attended Mr. Bosarge's funeral.

2—The Refugees

In a series of interviews with the authors, Heang Chhun recounted his harrowing escape from Cambodia and his subsequent immigration to the United States. Yang Yath, a Cambodian grandmother, did the same during an interview on May 10, 2007. Roy Hoffman of the *Mobile Register* wrote two splendid articles on Asian refugees in the Bayou area, both of which later appeared in his 2001 book *Back Home: Journeys through Mobile*. The stories in these pages of Kan Ly and Khampou

Phetsinorath were based primarily on Hoffman's accounts. The unattributed quotes regarding negative reactions to the Asian refugees were offered in interviews with the authors, as was Rodney Lyons's respectful and far more typical assessment of the Asians' contributions to the life and economy of the area.

Father Bieu Nguyen, priest at St. Margaret's Church, shared his thoughts on the refugee experience during an interview on October 5, 2006. On multiple occasions the authors have attended the Blessing of the Fleet ceremony and witnessed the participation of all the Bayou's ethnic groups. Joey Nguyen shared his family's story in an interview with the authors during the fall of 2006, as did Christy Te. Tran Nguyen and her father Truat Nguyen spoke at length with us in the summer of 2007. We also relied on interviews with Sophol and Chandara Ngam and the members of their family; with Mrs. Koan Ang, a Bayou translator, educator, and activist; and with Sue Chanthapaseuth, a caseworker for Boat People S.O.S. Chanthapaseuth spoke both about the problems faced by Asian young people in the Bayou area and about the warm welcome she and her own family have received.

Robert Shipp, chair of marine sciences at the University of South Alabama, offered his overview of the Bayou economy during interviews in the fall of 2006 and the summer of 2007. *Mobile Register* reporter Russ Henderson wrote extensively about Tim James's development plans for the Bayou, beginning in March 2005. His overview story, "Bayou nouveau," appeared on May 1, 2005.

3 — Katrina

Historian Douglas Brinkley wrote extensively about Hurricane Katrina in his book *The Great Deluge: Hurricane Katrina, New Orleans, and the Mississippi Gulf Coast*, and his account helps provide a backdrop for this chapter, as does the very detailed account in *Wikipedia*, the free online encyclopedia, which provided some of the meteorological detail. We also relied on the detailed coverage in the *Mobile Register*, produced by a team of excellent reporters, including Russ Henderson, Roy Hoffman, Rena Havner, Casandra Andrews, Penelope McClenny, and others.

Loan Vo recounted the story of her own family's ordeal, both in interviews with the authors and in a paper she wrote at Alba Middle School. Mary Wilkerson shared the video she took of the storm from the vantage point of her family's shrimp boat. Nancy McCall's memories of her pastor Will Prichard's sermons about the storm of 1906 were offered in interviews with the authors.

Tulane historian Lawrence Powell's paper on Katrina was presented at the Howard Mahan Symposium, sponsored by the University of South Alabama, March 7–10, 2007. The image of President George W. Bush flying over the devastation of New Orleans was based on an account in *The Great Deluge*, as was the summary of FEMA's incompetence in New Orleans. FEMA's delays in delivering trailers to hurricane victims in the Bayou were recounted in Russ Henderson's story in the *Mobile Register*, "Hurricane Victims Waiting for Housing," October 19, 2005.

Amber Hill's paper about her hurricane experience was written for her teachers at Alma Bryant High School. Her memories of drives along Coden beach with members of her family were recounted in interviews with the authors.

Over a period of several weeks, beginning on November 23, 2005, the *Mobile Register* reported on the saga of FEMA's refusal to help rescue grounded shrimp boats without charging the boat owners up to sixty thousand dollars. Mayor Stan

Wright's quote "It's awful" appeared in the *Register* on November 23. The quotes from the paper's editorial board—"Why are we not surprised?"—and from FEMA's Mike Bolch appeared on December 26. Building inspector Tommy Reynoso's quote "The Bayou still has a long way to go" appeared on September 24, 2006.

Coden activist Barbara Reid's words of appreciation to volunteers who poured in after the storm were published in *The Bayou Anthology*. Grace Scire recounted her experiences as a volunteer—and later as a staff member at Dr. Regina Benjamin's clinic—in a series of interviews with the authors beginning in the fall of 2006 and continuing into the spring and summer of 2007. Dr. Benjamin's story was beautifully told in the February 2006 *Reader's Digest*, as well as a number of other publications, including *Good Housekeeping*, *Redbook*, *Coastal Living*, *People*, the *Mobile Register*, and the *Journal of American History*. We also interviewed her for this book and Frye Gaillard wrote a chapter about her in the book *American Crisis: Southern Solutions*, published in 2008 by NewSouth Books. Nell Stoddard's quote "Here we go again" appeared in the *Reader's Digest* profile by Lynn Rosellini. Grace Scire's anecdote about Benjamin paying the pharmaceutical bills of her neediest patients came from an interview with the authors. The same story was told in *Reader's Digest*. Benjamin's quote, "We'll rebuild it," appeared in the *Mobile Register* on December 31, 2005. The article was written by Penelope McClenny.

In an interview with the authors in the summer of 2007, Mike Dillaber of Volunteer Mobile described his role in coordinating recovery efforts in the Bayou. The figures on federal aid to the area appeared in the *Mobile Register* on June 19, 2006. Coden activists Barbara Reid, Nancy McCall, and Ernestine Williams described their frustrations with the recovery process in interviews with the authors. The account of Reid's testimony before the Mobile County Commission appeared in the *Register* on November 10, 2006.

4—The Long Road Back

Peter F. Alba and Alma Bryant were both profiled in a Bayou La Batre bicentennial edition of the *Mobile County News*, October 16, 1986. The quote about Miss Bryant from Bun Stork, "She would whip your butt," came from a conversation with the authors at a Floyd Bosarge fish fry. Hope Bosarge's quote appeared in the *Mobile County News*. The Katrina photographs taken by Bayou students all appear in the publication *Eyes of the Storm: A Community Survives after Katrina*. The quotes from Adrian Overstreet and Mui Lam were found on CNN.com.

The *Mobile Register* recounted the demolition of downtown buildings in Bayou La Batre on March 7, 2007. Nell Bosarge Stoddard's lament came in an interview with the authors, shortly after that demolition. Jana Jowers wrote about the death of her cousin Charles Davis Nelson in a paper at Alba Middle School. A touching tribute to the talented young photographer Jada Davis, who was hit and killed by a car in September 2006, appears in *Eyes of the Storm*.

Grace Scire's observations about the resiliency of Bayou La Batre people and the potential dangers of another hurricane were offered in a series of interviews with the authors. Regina Benjamin's fact-finding trip to Thailand, which also included Tom Davis, executive director of the Community Foundation of South Alabama, was funded by the Ford Foundation; Benjamin explained the purpose of that journey in an interview with the authors. Larry Roberts recounted his harrowing story of survival, and his personal disagreements with the mayor, in an interview with the authors. Russ Henderson's story about Hung Nguyen, who could not understand a police warning to evacuate his home, appeared in the *Mobile Register* on May 29, 2006. Building inspector Tommy Reynoso summarized the Bayou's latest housing plans in an interview during the summer of 2007.

The *Mobile Register* provided extensive coverage of Tim James's development plans for the Bayou. The quote from Bayou shrimper Doug Johnson appeared in the paper on March 30, 2005; from Cyndi Johnson on May 1, 2005; and the exchange between James and Bayou resident Charlie Durden was quoted in the *Register* on July 14, 2005. The paper also covered the heated meeting of January 12, 2006, regarding a proposal to rezone the Bayou's waterfront. Mayor Stan Wright's opposition to the proposal was recounted in that article. The quote from a Bayou business owner, "There would have been some killing," occurred in a conversation with the authors.

The *Register* offered extensive coverage of the Urban Land Institute's recommendations for the Bayou, as did the Public Affairs Research Council of Louisiana in its extensive report in 2007 on recovery efforts all along the Gulf Coast. Mayor Stan Wright's quote, "Tim's not going to be in the driver's seat anymore," appeared in the *Register* on October 8, 2006, as did the potential comparison between Bayou La Batre and Santa Fe, and the quote from Bayou resident Kathy Gazzier. The article, entitled "Old Gulf Coast vs. New Gulf Coast" and written by Russ Henderson, also offered an in-depth comparison between the experiences of Bayou La Batre and Carrabelle, Florida, a fishing village that is also trying to reach out to tourists.

The story of Coden was pieced together from news coverage of the area, from conversations with schoolteachers and volunteers who have worked closely with the people, and from extensive conversations with local activists, including Nancy McCall, Barbara Reid, Edwina Bates, and others. The Public Affairs Research Council of Louisiana also reported on the deep frustrations of Coden's residents.

The story of the artists' colonies that thrived in the Bayou La Batre–Coden area from the 1930s to the 1950s was recounted in detail in Lynn Williams's article "Another Provincetown? Alabama's Gulf Coast Art Colonies at Bayou La Batre and Coden," which appeared in the *Gulf South Historical Review* in the spring of 2000.

The quote from painter Genevieve Southerland, "Spring has come to Bayou La Batre," appeared in that article. The word picture of painters working on "the 'oxbow' curves of the river bank" was written by Williams.

Robert Shipp of the University of South Alabama provided the closing summary on Bayou La Batre's economy, and Lisa Creal and Tyler Kittles both offered their thoughts on life in the Bayou in separate interviews with the authors. Mayor Stan Wright offered his overview in an interview with Frye Gaillard on July 17, 2007.

Appendix—Bayou Voices

The excerpt from Julian Lee Rayford's *Whistlin' Woman and Crowin' Hen* is taken from pages 24–25 of that book. The granite marker at St. Margaret's Catholic Church, which contains a prayer for the fishing fleet, is located next to the church's dock on the eastern shore of the bayou itself. Alma Bryant's long essay on the hurricane of 1906, excerpted briefly here, appears in full in *The Bayou Anthology*. Rodney Lyons's description of Miss Bryant and her brother George Bryant making gumbo was offered in an interview with Sheila Hagler in 2001. Miller Johnson's recollections of his Heron Bay boyhood appear in full in *The Bayou Anthology*. The concluding quote, "I'd rather tong oysters than be president of the United States," first appeared in Russ Henderson's "The Heron Bay way," in the November 5, 2006, *Mobile Register*.

The descriptions of Bayou La Batre and Coden, published in a pamphlet by the Works Progress Administration around the time of World War II, also appear in Lynn Williams's article "Another Provincetown? Alabama's Gulf Coast Art Colonies at Bayou La Batre and Coden," published in the spring 2000 issue of the *Gulf South Historical Review*. Peggy Denniston's essay on Hurricane Katrina appears in the book *Eyes of the Storm: A Community Survives after Katrina*, which was published in 2006 and contains poetry and photographs by students at Alba Middle School and Elm Place Middle School in Highland Park, Illinois. Jada Davis's poem "Katrina's Pain" appeared in that same publication, as does Saphea Khan's "Five Thousand Dollars."

In an interview with the authors in 2007, Elsie Simmons offered her thoughts about Katrina's effect on the African American community in Coden. Phillip Morris told his story in a taped interview with his daughter-in-law, Sandra Morris. The excerpt here is used with permission. Jimmy Wigfield's powerful memoir about his father first appeared in the *Mobile Register*, and Tyler Kittles's analysis of his hometown, written during the summer and fall of 2007, was part of a creative writing project at the University of South Alabama. Koan Ang and Sue Chanthapaseuth spoke at length about Bayou La Batre in conversations with the authors. Joey Nguyen's paper about the promising beauty of a Bayou sunset, written at Alma Bryant High School before he graduated in 2006, offers, we think, the perfect metaphor for the hope that survives in this part of the world.

In addition to those people who have shared their stories, we also want to thank Clarence Mohr, chair of the history department at the University of South Alabama, for encouraging this project, and Dale Foster, former director of the Daphne Public Library, who first suggested a book on Bayou La Batre. Thanks also to Michelle Cagle and Debbie Thomaston at the University of South Alabama for their patience, good humor, and logistical help. We appreciate the support of Mark Wilson and Jay Lamar at the Caroline Marshall Draughon Center for the Arts and Humanities at Auburn University, as well as Dan Ross and Dan Waterman of the University of Alabama Press. And special thanks, finally, to Nancy Gaillard, who read and responded to the manuscript, and to Amy Rogers, who brought her keen editor's eye to the project as it entered into its final stages. We are grateful to all.